Just How Far from the Apple Tree?

A Son in Relation to His Famous Father

John S. Peale

iUniverse, Inc.
Bloomington

Just How Far from the Apple Tree?
A Son in Relation to His Famous Father

iUniverse books may be ordered through booksellers or by contacting:

iUniverse
1663 Liberty Drive
Bloomington, IN 47403
www.iuniverse.com
1-800-Authors (1-800-288-4677)

Because of the dynamic nature of the Internet, any web addresses or links contained in this book may have changed since publication and may no longer be valid. The views expressed in this work are solely those of the author and do not necessarily reflect the views of the publisher, and the publisher hereby disclaims any responsibility for them.

Any people depicted in stock imagery provided by Thinkstock are models, and such images are being used for illustrative purposes only.

Certain stock imagery © Thinkstock.

ISBN: 978-1-4759-2622-4 (sc)
ISBN: 978-1-4759-2624-8 (hc)
ISBN: 978-1-4759-2623-1 (e)

Printed in the United States of America

iUniverse rev. date: 8/13/2012

To my two loving sisters,
Margaret Peale Everett and Elizabeth Peale Allen—

Who know both what it means,
And what it meant

Contents

Preface

F rom the perspective of my midseventies, I have a story to tell of my becoming, my personal development, in relation to my famous and much-beloved dad, Norman Vincent Peale. He was a man of vision and power as a preacher, public speaker, and writer. Possessing extraordinary talents and energy, he was an orator of the old school who could inspire and engage a congregation or audience with his distinctive outlook on life, not to mention his self-deprecating humor. He wrote an enormously influential book, *The Power of Positive Thinking*, and many other books, and he created a "practical Christianity," which he developed through the Christian church and years of successful publishing and business endeavors. My mother, Ruth Stafford Peale, herself a highly talented person, dedicated her life to the one task of creating the maximum conditions for her husband to be at his most focused, creative, and productive best. Throughout my life I have had a healthy and sincere respect for both my dad and my mother.

I am the son—brother to two caring sisters—who had to find my own way in a kind of home, family, and cultural environment which goes with the situation of having such a famous father. My story is one of the ways of my becoming what I am today, through a happy childhood and extensive education, followed by a successful career as a professor of philosophy. More importantly, in my middle years, I lived through personal tension, struggle, darkness, and despair to emerge happily to where I am today—*in the Sunlight of the Spirit.*

Acknowledgments

There are special people I wish to thank for reading my manuscript and for making numerous suggestions, corrections, or comments. They are my loving wife, Lydia, and my good friend Stephen Pfleiderer, a former professional editor and currently a writing coach. Also, I would like to thank my two sisters, Margaret and Elizabeth, and my three children, Laura, Clifford, and Lacy, each of whom has read the entire manuscript, has gotten caught up in it, and has suffered with it and made helpful suggestions. These caring people have worked hard with and for me to help make my book a better one. The editorial team at iUniverse, especially George Nedeff and Jan Ley, have been of enormous help in making this book what it is today. I also want to thank my good friend Doug Campbell for reading and critically evaluating the manuscript. Of course, I alone am responsible for my personal opinions and feelings expressed about my dad and my mother. Any defects in the book that remain are on my own plate.

Introduction

Generally, this is a book for those who have had concerns about their relations with their parents, particularly men in relation to their fathers. I am such a person, and my primary focus is my relation to my dad. Another major focus is my becoming, my psychological and spiritual development to what I am today. It is my hope that this book may be of interest and provide hope to those who feel the need to think about their own relations to their father or parents. Perhaps my story will allow others to see more clearly their own situations. In telling about my life in relation to my dad, I am also telling my personal story, seeking for the reader to get to know me as a person, so that a clear comparison can be made to my dad in order to judge just how far I am from the apple tree.

At three points between my chapters on the modes or ways of my becoming, I present interludes, as if they were pauses between the acts of a dramatic play. In these, I seek to present my dad and his point of view, to give my introduction of him and show how I felt about him, how much love I have had for him.

This book is also directed to my own family—that is, my wife and three children and their spouses and children. It is also written for the families of my two sisters, Margaret Peale Everett, whom I call Maggie, and Elizabeth Peale Allen, whom I call Eliz. Everyone in the greater Peale family, at one time or another, has found their own relations to Norman Vincent Peale and to Ruth Stafford Peale to be a matter of importance or concern. Certainly, this relation has been a "thing" to deal with. Perhaps working through my story will be a help to my family members in thinking through their own relations with the two people so important to the lives of all of us.

In this book, *I relate what has been going on in me as I have sought to find my way in relation to my dad.* It is also about how I found what I had been seeking since I was a young man—a resolution of the tension in me between being so near to him and yet so separated. There has been a paradox in my life, stated as a question: how could I be close to my dad and also be disconnected from him? It seems that this paradox has been a major cause of tumult in my life. Yet seemingly miraculously, in my seventies, there has come to me a peaceful and creative response to the nearly lifelong agonizing and disturbing conflicts within me. The personal paradox has been largely resolved. As my story unfolds, I will be probing the issue of what caused these conflicts, factors that contributed to it, perhaps even a root cause. We'll be doing this together with the more important issue of how I was able to get beyond them.

In my life, I have been seeking to find my own way, apart from the force and image of my dad in my life. This search has been *the single most important factor in my life.* The effort of finding my way has finally come to a distinctively contented conclusion in a new state of my being. The journey has been a painful one, taking me along pathways of counseling and recovery from darkness, despair, and alcoholism, all of which will be detailed toward the end of the book. In all of this, I have gained understanding and insight. I've sought out what I was to become, what I wanted to be, and what I felt that I should be. In the end, miraculously, I have come to see and feel the Sunlight of the Spirit.

Throughout most of my life, the seeming omnipresence of my dad—that is, the disturbing power of my image of him—has inspired, impressed, and made me proud, but it has also haunted, driven, challenged, angered, and depressed me down into the depths.

Now in my midseventies, I have found the peace I have searched for over many decades, and I'm in a contented state with regard to my past and with my often vivid memories of good and bad times in my life. Memories and the way we feel about them have a nontemporal character in that they are of the past but also in the present. Selected specific memories of my past consciously and unconsciously shape my present consciousness and my hopes for the future. I am not writing this book as an autobiography, where memories would be related sequentially from birth to old age. As the chapter titles suggest, I am recounting different modes or ways of my becoming, my personal development to what I now am. The reader should not expect to discover a chronological presentation of key points in my life.

What follows are like the scenes of a theatre play, revealing the various aspects of my personal development. In such dramatic plays, we see the sides of the character develop as the story unfolds, and so it will be with me. In my play, there are interludes, as if between scenes, that show how the relation between me and my dad is full of love and respect and also struggle and pain.

Taken together, my memories constitute a collection of important recollections of my past and my present that makes up what is me. There is a sense in which memories, especially the selective memories in my conscious mind, define who I am. Only I have this particular collection and arrangement of memories. In his *Essay Concerning Human Understanding*, John Locke took this position about personal identity. And it seems right for me.

Author's Note

My personal story has come to include the details about how I became an alcoholic, how it was with me, what happened to me, and what my life is like now. I recount my life in recovery in a twelve-step program. That story is told here openly and honestly and in considerable detail. I make little or no effort to soften or hide the truth of what happened to me during this difficult time of my life. In the text of this book, I will use quotations from the literature in a twelve-step program. For the sake of anonymity, I will not document these quotations. For the purpose of anonymity, I will substitute fictitious names for all other alcoholics to whom I make reference. Those who read this book will realize that I am an enthusiastic fan of the North Carolina Tar Heels men's basketball program and that I have been a student of the Bible most of my life. The fictitious names I choose will be taken from my list of Tar Heel all-stars and from the leading characters in the Bible.

Becoming

What to me does becoming me mean? It means that I have been able to develop personally. It means that what has been potential in me has to some good extent become actual. More specifically, it means that throughout my life up until my seventies, there has been within me a basic personal and foundational tension, always with the hope for a possible resolution. I have lived between finding my own way and following my dad; between having had a close personal connection with him but losing it and never finding it again; between finding my own niche, my talents, passions, and commitments, yet struggling with those that have come from him.

The resolution of this basic tension in me always seemed merely possible. Interestingly, in a video clip of my dad preaching long ago, I noticed that he defined "possible" according to the fourth meaning in *Merriam Webster's Dictionary*: "able to become into being." I have been able to become into my being. This indicates the whole direction of this book.

This basic tension in my soul, both a positive and negative factor in my life, has stimulated me and pulled me forward. It also has frustrated me and held me back in my life and work. Because of it, I have been motivated to work things out for myself, both personally and academically. Yet, also due to this tension, I have been tied up in emotional knots and thus not as clearly focused in my life and work. Due to it, I sought ways of release from these emotional states that caused me to lose concentration and a relaxed sense of knowing that I was on the right track.

Thus, becoming has come to mean this: to live and work through this conflict and to come out to my being now to a personal place to which the ancient Chinese philosopher Confucius came in his seventies. Due to his clear focus on learning since he was fifteen, Confucius developed the good discipline in life and the good habits in his learning that enabled him to come to a point where he could do as he pleased and also could give his "heart-mind free rein" and yet not overstep the mark for his high calling.

This process has stages of different modes or ways that becoming has been manifest in my life. These modes are indicated in the table of contents. Each of the three interludes is placed where it is, and its content fits in with the stages of becoming. There is a rhythm to these modes of becoming and interludes as the process works itself out to the culmination of being me.

Perhaps an analogy would help. In classical musical compositions, there are sometimes lines of dissonant musical themes in minor keys resolving, sometimes at the end of a piece, into a harmony in the major voice. When I speak of music, I have in mind classical music, such as symphonies and piano sonatas of Beethoven or operas, say, of Wagner. I received counsel on this matter from Michelle Krisel, General Director of Ash Lawn Opera in Charlottesville, Virginia, where we live and where I serve on the Ash Lawn Opera board. Michelle points out that musical dissonances resolve, yet these are not the same as the shift from minor to major keys. Minor is not a dissonance; it's a color. So the shift from minor to major signifies a shift from dark/sad to happy/light. The resolution of dissonance feels like the shift from complication/uncertainty to clarity/peace. In my life, I have experienced both the shifts from minor to major keys and the resolution of dissonance as Michelle describes.

She and I talked about the music of Beethoven, how in his pieces in which he uses sonata forms, he has all sorts of developments between themes with such nuances as she suggested. Beethoven is not known for his shifts from minor to major, but rather he develops his themes—plays with them, makes them more complicated, and regards them from all angles—before resolving them. She also pointed out Richard Wagner's *Tristan und Isolde*. At the grand climax in the final scene, Isolde gazes upon her dead lover, Tristan, believing that he is awakening to a new life. She believes she will unite with him in death through her certain belief that their love is immortal. This is the famous "Liebestod" or "love death." There was a death in love between me and my dad as we got personally disconnected in the course of our lives.

It is my fervent hope that there may still be a full resolution in the life to come. This is what I affirmed in the last sentence of my talk at his memorial service. I sincerely affirm that hope.

Chapter 1: Becoming in Loving and Being Loved

In my life, I have enjoyed the good fortune of loving my dad and having been loved by him from boyhood days through to his death on December 24, 1993, at the age of ninety-five. I have loved both my parents similarly. This constant love has enabled me to have personal development in my life, an important mode of my becoming. My dad and mother loved me and my two sisters, Maggie and Eliz. Under the influence of such a loving beginning in life, we three children, now grandparents, have had the blessing of becoming so loving and so personally close all our lives.

Parental love, as I remember it, was more often shown rather than told. It was more clearly shown to me and my sisters when my parents weren't so busy, especially when they could take us on trips with them. They were busily occupied much of the time. During the late 1930s and 1940s, our dad was engaged in an extensive schedule of speaking engagements around the country, establishing a ministry to business and professional groups. Also, he started writing such books as *The Art of Living* and *A Guide to Confident Living*. He was making for himself a widening sphere of influence and a growing reputation. His reputation would soar even higher after the publication of *The Power of Positive Thinking* in 1952. We three kids were born during the 1930s and early 1940s—Maggie in 1933, me in 1936, and Eliz in 1942. His message to his speaking and reading audiences was resonating with increasing intensity, especially in and soon after World War II. During these years in our family, there was love and caring, but not so much attention from our extremely busy dad, who was becoming famous and in demand.

In the 1940s, there were two places our family traveled to in the summers when Dad was on his annual three-month vacation from the Marble Collegiate Church in New York City. We went to the Mountain View House in Whitefield, New Hampshire, and the Mohonk Mountain House on a ridge above New Paltz, New York. We would do things as a family, and our parents were with us, having fun and loving times together. Mother and Dad would play games with us inside on the chess or checkers boards, or in the room with a pool table, or in the dining room while having dinners together. They often tolerated and even enjoyed the pranks we kids played on each other, like the time Maggie filled my glass with buttermilk, which I hated, and then challenged me to a milk-drinking contest. There was also the time when I, like a gentleman, pulled out the dining room chair for her to be seated. When she started to sit, I first drew the chair in and then pulled it out quickly so that she ended up on the floor!

I remember many fun and memorable summers and other vacation times at Quaker Hill, a community above Pawling, New York, where we had a second home. My parents bought the eighteen-acre property back in the winter of 1944. Dad named this place Sugar Tree Farm, after a location of a church in southern Ohio, near where his father served his first pastorate in a Methodist church a long time ago. At Quaker Hill, my two sisters and I had a happy life with Mother and Dad. We had lots of relaxed and downtime with our parents. I remember picking peaches from the orchard and making homemade ice cream, and picking fresh strawberries for breakfast from the garden.

It was at the Quaker Hill Country Club—the "Barn" as it was affectionately known—where we played golf and tennis, had square dances, put on funny skits, and had interesting programs. One memorable program, for example, was that given by Lowell Thomas of "so-long-until-tomorrow" fame. There he talked about his time with T. E. Lawrence or "Lawrence of Arabia," showing us artifacts he had brought back from the Middle East. Lawrence has been of interest to me ever since. Even recently, I have been doing extensive reading about his life and his work, *Seven Pillars of Wisdom*.

At home, we had memorable, active family dinners where we talked and kidded around. While there on one of Dad's birthdays, I gave him a card with a swashbuckling figure on the front. It read: "Here is a 24 cents birthday card." On the inside, it said: "I give no quarter on an occasion such as this." Dad loved it and laughed heartily. My sisters and I remember all of these kinds of times with fondness and pleasure. The happy and memorable experiences in my boyhood helped me develop into what I am today.

We had many trips with our family. One memorable trip was during a summer when we took an extended Pullman train trip around many of the splendid sites in the West, such as Yellowstone and Glacier National Parks, the Grand Tetons, and the large redwood trees in the Northwest. Especially fun was the nighttime activity in our Pullman drawing room, where we all slept, and where my sisters and I would swing like monkeys from berth to berth, especially on the upper levels. These were loving and happy times in the family.

There were good family times for all of us, including birthdays, graduations, and the like. And so it was with holidays like Christmas and Thanksgiving—all happy times, as I remember. One Christmas, a sour note came to Elizabeth when she received the gift of a bottle of deodorant from our mother. She was perplexed by the mixed message. As the years passed, such occasions for our own children were special, and Mother and Dad entered in with enthusiasm, most of the time.

An example of Dad's love and acceptance of me was when he received a letter from a dean at Washington and Lee University, where I was a student. The dean wrote about my singing in a Christmas service in an Episcopal church on Washington Street in Lexington, Virginia. I was singing "O Little Town of Bethlehem." Dad read the letter at a family dinner, showing obvious love and respect on his face as he read the beautifully phrased description of my dulcet tones and my religious feeling expressed in the singing. As I look back now at this incident, I can see that his love was entwined with approval.

I was constantly seeking signs of his approval, and I always had the uncomfortable feeling of having to earn this approval to get his love. Earning that approval came to be more and more problematic as the years went by, and I even felt the love became more questionable. The realization that I had to earn his and mother's approval came slowly into my consciousness during high school and my college years. As will become very clear later on, the realization that I had not met their approval—most importantly, my dad's—came about the time that I decided to become a philosophy major at Washington and Lee University.

When I came to that point, I started to realize even more that I was experiencing a large part of the significant loss of personal contact with him that I suffered with for the rest of my life, until just recently. I do not believe that my sisters experienced their relations with our parents—especially our dad—in the same way. Emotionally, the growing realization of this loss of connection with my dad felt terrible, like a hole in my gut, an emptiness in my heart that hurt badly. As my life developed, anger came upon me, gnawing away at me and further distracting me from peace and a clear sense of purpose. Living with that emptiness was a factor that held me back in what became my life's pursuit.

In 1972, when I made a speech from the public pulpit on the occasion of his fortieth anniversary as Minister of Marble Collegiate Church, he came as close as he ever would in telling me that he loved me. On that occasion, I told him of my love and respect. As I look back on that occasion, I am reminded of how rare such outright expressions of his love and respect to me were. These mutual expressions occurred in a public and "special" occasion. It did not happen in the everyday setting, and it did not erase or heal the gnawing emptiness and frustration in my heart.

Chapter 2: Becoming in Excitement about Life

⁓

As I write this section, I am anticipating the performance of Rossini's *The Barber of Seville* by our local opera company in Charlottesville, Virginia, named Ash Lawn Opera. This reminds me of when I was young, swelling with excited appreciation of diverse and interesting cultural events so readily available in New York City. I recall the singing of the accomplished and powerful Jussi Bjorling in Carnegie Hall, as I did when I heard *Aida* at the Old Metropolitan Opera building on Broadway and Thirty-Ninth Street. I recall being so impressed with the singing and dancing of Ray Bolger on the Broadway stage, singing "Once in Love with Amy." I remember seeing the original Broadway productions of *South Pacific* with Ezio Pinza singing "Some Enchanted Evening" and *The Sound of Music* with Mary Martin singing "Climb Every Mountain." I was becoming a person who enjoyed these sorts of cultural excitements. My personal development has continued with this sort of enrichment to the present day.

All my life, I have read books, taught books, written books, remembering all the while how, as a school boy, I felt my first love of books and records. I remember being so absorbed and caught up in the *Bounty Trilogy: Mutiny on the Bounty, Men against the Sea* and *Pitcairn's Island* by Charles Nordhoff and James Norman Hall. I remember my first year at Deerfield Academy in a study hall, reading James Hilton's *Lost Horizon* and being chided by a study hall proctor, who had a glint in his eye as he suggested that I ought to be doing my homework instead.

To him, I said, "Sir, I can't put this book down. I'll do my homework when I am finished." He walked away, having made his point but with a knowing, appreciative smile, recognizing the point that I had made.

In middle school, I remember coming home from the Friends Seminary School on Eighteenth Street, at Rutherford Place between Second and Third Avenues, while eating my jujubes and kidding around with my friend Peter. I would often stop and browse in the original Barnes & Noble bookstore on the way to our apartment at Forty-Fifth Avenue, only a few blocks away. I dreamed of having a big library of my own one day. Today I find it difficult to find specific books I want to consult in our library of over ten thousand books, many of which, in our retirement, are in a self-storage unit. When I was still a boy, my parents noticed that I was spending all my extra money on books and records while I had holes in my shoes. My mother bought shoes for me, but I guess she was wondering about my values. Regarding my personal spending, my heart was more in my mind than my feet. It still is.

I do not remember either of my parents having that kind of love of books and learning. Dad did have worn-out books of English poets, such as William Wordsworth. He quoted poetry quite often and other works of significant writers, such as Marcus Aurelius, Ralph Waldo Emerson, and William James. As I remember it, however, these references were not given as an expression of the love of literature or learning but as useful and important points in his sermons and his writing. Besides, Dad was always too busy with his work to be delayed long in reading and study. I always thought that Mother would exercise her wider interests in culture and learning, but that never seemed to happen. For Dad, reading was sometimes an escape from his work, as when he pored over stories of the Old West by Louis L'Amour.

Work for Dad was something he did constantly and thought about when he wasn't actually doing it. Work consisted of preaching, administering his church as the chairman of the governing board, writing speeches, writing books, and reading to get information and stories about the practical difficulties of people so that he could apply the principles of the Christian faith to form ideas that could be of help in solving these debilitating and frustrating personal problems. During his career, he wrote forty-six books and many pamphlets and booklets. He also composed and delivered a very large number of sermons from the 1920s to his retirement in 1984. His last public address was in the fall of 1992. He was a popular and much-beloved public figure.

I have emphasized cultural excitements that I have enjoyed all my life. Beneath these specific feelings lies a general personal attitude toward life, that of getting involved and personally excited and engaged in many things. When I was teaching, my college students used to talk of being bored, and I always wondered what that was like. From my dad and mother, we three kids certainly got a vital sense of the excitements and interests in life.

When on the trips I mentioned above—those to the New Hampshire Mountain View House or the Mohonk Mountain House or to the Western Rockies—our parents always showed us a love of nature and the great outdoors. We have a granddaughter named Rachel whom we kid when we are taken by a beautiful scene in nature, for she doesn't yet find this engaging. But Lydia and I do find such things important, and we have been fortunate to have traveled so widely and to have experienced interesting and beautiful places in the world. In our lives together, we find such a rich pattern of shared interests and commitments, and we have such a wide variety of pleasures in similar and interestingly different pursuits. Closeness as so described has come out clearly on our travels, concerning literature, history, and international relations related to specific places we have traveled, especially in China.

Such an attitude has carried Lydia and me forward through our marriage of fifty-one years in a zest for living. There are places that are so special to us both in our loving times together, such as the downtown mall in Charlottesville near where we live, or the Outer Banks of North Carolina, where we have a home on the beach just north of the village of Duck. At the beach, it is such a good day, which can begin by seeing the "Big Show" of the sunrise over the Eastern horizon early in the morning. To the west, the day can end with visions of the setting sun over the sound in Currituck County. Walking along the Downtown Mall of our city of Charlottesville, Virginia, or getting going in the early morning at the beach can come alive with the Glory of God any time of day or night. Such are everyday kinds of special times in our long, happy marriage together.

On a typical good day at the beach on the Outer Banks, we will take walks, sensing the power and beauty of varying colors of the water, and notice shapes of things the sea has deposited on the beach. We notice the seagulls and the sandpipers and an occasional school of dolphins. We will take afternoon naps, opening the door so that we can hear the sound of the sea crashing on the beach. And we will go to our several fine restaurants, such as The Blue Point or Fin and Claw, enjoying fresh local seafood and the abundantly subtle tastes and textures of the food well prepared in these favorite eating establishments. We have come to know and share much of life with the chefs and waitstaff at these restaurants, several of whom have become good friends over the years.

Of course, either at our home in Charlottesville or at our beach home on North Carolina's Outer Banks, Lydia and I love to enjoy the company of our three children and five grandchildren. Most every summer, our entire family comes to be with us at the beach, and we revel in the good life of relaxation and fun together.

There are many other things that are of considerable interest to us, such as political rallies, debates, and elections. For years, we have been active in political affairs and have worked the polls or other activities at election times. Then there are the memorable times, such as when our son Clifford came into our bedroom at 1:39 in the morning of Election Day in 1976 to tell us that Jimmy Carter had taken California, that his election seemed imminent.

I am so interested in learning of my dad's lifelong interest in politics as I read biographies and critical studies of his life before I was born and before I knew so much about what he did. Perhaps it was a sign of things to come, for in the first election in which I voted, my ballot was cast for Richard Nixon on the Republican ticket. I was under the sway of the thinking of my parents. That was the only time, however, that I voted Republican. I never realized the extent of Dad's involvement with politics in his early life, and his considerations as to whether that was or was not a good thing for him to do as a minister of the gospel.

After I voted for Richard Nixon in my first presidential election, I came to take the other side politically, and soon after, I switched my allegiance to the Democrats, for whom I have worked and campaigned ever since. When I read about his early political involvement, I came to understand even more strongly how much he was on the other side of the political spectrum from me, especially in sentiments in favor of prohibition and against communism and Cold War conservatism, such as one finds in the career of his friend J. Edgar Hoover. When I read about his and Dad's involvements in the forties and early fifties, I was not surprised.

What has meant so much to me over the years is an attitude of mind and heart, a sense of the vitality of life and engagement with it. This is what I mean by "excitement about life." So much of this was inherited from my dad. Even if I was on the other side of him when it came to involvements in society and culture and education, I shared with him a zest and an enthusiasm for living, for doing good work helpful to people, and for taking stands on current issues of the day. This attitude of involvement and engagement has been a major factor in my becoming.

Chapter 3: Becoming in Inspiration and Illumination in My Religious Faith

◦∿◦

I do not remember becoming religious or being converted and becoming a Christian. For me, there was not an initial and life-changing religious experience. I was a religious person and a Christian boy growing up in a Christian family. We had Christian observances and Christian patterns of behavior naturally and regularly most every day. Dad would pray at any time, at any place, extemporaneously and naturally, and seemingly with no preparation and no hint of formality. Oh, how I admired this! He offered prayers for personal occasions for each of us children all through our early lives. Of course, there were blessings before meals and religious services in church regularly, all of which inspired in me a sense of the presence of God and what my parents called "the life-saving presence of the Lord Jesus Christ." An important factor in my becoming or personal development has been the maintenance and growth of my religious sense and, specifically, my Christian commitment in my life and work.

When I was a boy sitting with the family in the "pastor's pew" at Marble Collegiate Church, I would look up to the pulpit and see my dad and listen to him; I was swelled with pride. He was an old-fashioned orator type of preacher. It is reported that as a boy in Ohio, he hid under platforms on which no less than William Jennings Bryan gave his orations in the early twentieth century. Perhaps Dad even practiced speaking by putting pebbles in his mouth like the ancient Greek Demosthenes!

When Dad prayed from the pulpit at Marble, he would include a period of silence so that we, the congregation silently included, would pray with him. With this, there was in me a palpable religious sense. In later life when I was filled with the Spirit of God, I would pray—or try to pray well—like he did. But I felt that I was more forced and guarded in my praying, not opening as easily as Dad did to the Spirit of God in prayer. The naturalness of his praying style in public is what impressed me most.

All of this was a major inspiration for me to go into the ministry, which I did, and in preparation for this, I went to theological seminary. I sought and gained ordination in the Reformed Church in America, known also as the Dutch Reformed Church. I was ordained in a service in Marble Collegiate Church, with Dad presiding. Again I swelled up with pride as he gave the ministerial charge to me as a candidate for ordination. I felt his approval that day. This is not to say that I went into the ministry just to get that approval, but I did relish it when I got it. On that occasion, I thought about how it must have been for him as his minister father, Charles Clifford Peale, gave his son, Norman, the charge. I remembered that it was in Marble Church that Grandpa Peale baptized me, with my proud parents holding me, the baby.

As I look back on my ordination, I see how important it is to me. In this case, my dad was with me just as a father. Later, I realized that this symbolic meaning got lost, particularly after my dad's greater fame set in, especially after the publication of *The Power of Positive Thinking* in 1952 during the middle of my high school years. Later, however, I came to admire my paternal grandfather, so that also gave symbolic meaning to the baptism event. I was proud as I represented the continuance of a tradition from Charles Clifford, through Norman Vincent, and to me. That pride continued when Lydia and I named our own son Charles Clifford Peale, after his great-grandfather.

In my own way, I have tried to make my whole life a ministry. It has always been one in which I have been seeking to be a vehicle for that Spirit of God, which I first got from my parents, to flow through me out to other people. In this, I was able to get out of myself and think of others. This has become so important in my becoming, my spiritual development, and life through all my years.

In my study and intellectual work throughout my life, I have often stressed themes in religious experience and spirituality. In college, I read and absorbed *Mysticism* by Evelyn Underhill, illuminated in my mind and heart by her discussion of the stages of the mystic way, and especially by her material on Teresa of Avila and St. John of the Cross. In graduate school, I devoured William James's book *The Varieties of Religious Experience,* setting aside everything for a time, just as I set aside my homework at Deerfield to read *Lost Horizon.*

In Boston University's Directed Study courses, I studied one-on-one with Professor Amiya Chakravarty, who had been a personal secretary to the Indian poet Tagore and also a teacher of Martin Luther King. Together we read the classic three-volume work entitled *Hinduism and Buddhism* by Sir Charles Eliot. With Chakravarty, I also digested the major work of the nineteenth-century Indian mystic Ramakrishna, and under Richard Millard, I wrote a master's thesis on The Mystic Way in St. John of the Cross and Ramakrishna.

Years later at Fordham University, I took a summer seminar for college teachers on "The Journey in Medieval Mysticism," with emphasis on such important figures as Augustine in his *Confessions* and Richard of Saint Victor in his *Mystical Ark.* That I connected with Ewert Cousins, the director of the seminar, was important to me then and now. His influence helped to fix in my mind and heart the mystical consciousness in the religious life. That has meant so much to me ever since my friendship with him blossomed in the early 1980s.

Throughout my life and teaching career, I have continued a life of spiritual contemplation, with worship and prayer and a sense of illumination and divine presence in my life and work. This has been an important constant with me over the years. For years, I have served as a minister on call in local churches, mostly in Virginia. I have preached and prayed, baptized and married, and always worshipped. Such a religious sense continues in me to this day, together with Lydia. Even as I write these words, I feel the Spirit.

Today I am actively engaged in our local church and related organizations and also political and cultural groups. Part of this, of course, comes from my zest for life, which comes from my dad, and I feel, as did he, an enthusiasm in being an active and involved member of the communities where I live. I enjoy being regarded as a leader and as a person who makes significant contributions to important organizations.

In connection with our religious lives, my wife, Lydia, and I have readings and prayers each evening together, and a good deal of our common life together is oriented to worship and seeking to be of service and help to those less fortunate and needy in our community. For us, this involves work with the homeless, which we do in connection with an organization known as PACEM—People and Congregations Engaged in Ministry—at our local church.

Chapter 4: Becoming in Sentimentality

M y dad was a sentimentalist. By this, I mean that he wore his feelings on his sleeve, naturally, with little or no put-ons or affectations. His feelings were obvious to all around him, though he always tried to present a *positive* sense in relation to others. It was his feelings, first and foremost, that had a determinative effect on the way he was and what he thought and did. The primary personal attitude leading, guiding, and directing him in his life was feeling.

It is interesting to me that my copy of the *Concise Oxford English Dictionary* defines "sentimental" as "deriving from feelings of tenderness, sadness or nostalgia—having or arousing such feelings in an exaggerated or self-indulgent way." The dictionary continues to define sentimental value, "value of an object deriving from personal or emotional associations rather than material worth."

The caveat of the dictionary's definition—"in an exaggerated or self-indulgent way"—was telling for my dad, as it has also been for me. Dad seemed to overplay the importance of how he felt about himself and how he felt about people in a given situation. In the words of my father-in-law, Dr. Edgar A. Woods, he was often, too often it seemed, "taking his emotional temperature." It was as if he was doing an emotional self-check all the time.

As I matured, it was also apparent to me that he was "self-indulgent," thinking about himself too much, putting too much of a sense of value on his feelings. As I read about Dad in his life before I knew him, it seems clear that his moods were mercurial, subject to dramatic fluctuations up and down as he adjusted to criticism or difficult experiences. For example, when criticized, such as he was when early on at Marble Collegiate Church he wanted to enlarge the choir from a quartet to a full chorus, he would sink into a despondent mood, thinking something was wrong with him. Such high and low mood swings certainly were his when criticized for his political involvements, such as his role on the Committee for Constitutional Government in the early 1940s. Such mood swings, as I have learned from my own experience in my personal development, stem from too much of a focus on myself and how I feel.

The history of Dad's life is replete with important references to and insights from his inferiority complex. In reading about his early life in magazine articles and biographies, I have learned that he was a shy, retiring, thin young man who was hesitant to express himself. This came out particularly in school, even into college and graduate school, when called upon in class to recite or to give his opinion. Two particular professors at his college, Ohio Wesleyan University, took him aside and gave him advice. They praised him for being the kind of student who has much to say but were puzzled as he was red-faced and embarrassed when asked to speak or express himself. One professor thought that he was too self-oriented, thinking of himself too much and not able to focus on whatever was the issue at hand.

Dad was a special person, with good insights and enormous talents. And as such, he must have thought well of himself. Perhaps he was an egotist with an inferiority complex. As I see it, a kind of selfishness and self-centeredness was part of his life and at the root of his problems. As I see it, these words also describe me. They have been with me in my going down in my life and then up in my recovery. In the addiction and recovery parts of this book, these emphases will be clear.

For a sentimentalist, there is an important sense that feelings and emotions come before thinking and thought, and that they have a power over our rationality. By "come before," I mean to suggest not preceding in time but in importance. I am reminded of the advice about writing— often given by teachers—that a first draft should come from the heart, with later revisions coming from the head. One can have a feeling sense about a situation or a person, about which the head may make revisions, but it is the former rather than the latter that moves or motivates a person to action. Feelings and emotions motivate; thought understands. So feelings and emotions have a power over our thinking.

For that to be said about Norman Vincent Peale, the positive thinker, is striking! As I understand positive thinking, the relation of thought to feeling is precisely opposite of what I have just described for the sentimentalist. In Dad's view of positive thinking, it is a thought that precedes feeling and emotions in importance and has power over them.

That said, however, I too, like my dad, basically feel my way into life situations, and *I am proud of it.* I have felt my way into life, looking to my feelings to sense how it is with me, what is going on around me. In many situations, I want to be sensitive about how I can best act toward or respond to other people. This is particularly true in cases where I would like to be of some help to others.

There are positive feelings in such sentimentality, for it can provide the basis of a sensitive, feeling approach to other people—being sensitive to their feelings and caring about their welfare. Such feelings help people open up to others and, in our contemporary way of speaking, "connect." My paternal grandfather, Charles Clifford Peale, was like this; he was able to get to know and relate to people easily and naturally. Dad was like this, and, hopefully, so am I. As I see it, this is something commendable.

There were times when Dad's sentimentality came to the fore. We were traveling as a family in the Rocky Mountains on a Pullman train, in the old days when the back of the last car was an open platform from which one could well capture a sense of the natural beauty of the mountain scenery. My sister Elizabeth, quite young then, lost her shoe off the open platform as the train chugged on. Dad displayed characteristic sentimentality as we went back to our compartment. He led the family in a feeling-oriented prayer for that little lost shoe. The sentiment was about the shoe, but mostly directed at Eliz, with the objective of comforting her. He also, perhaps, wanted to teach us the lesson that God can be present in any situation in our lives, no matter how seemingly small and insignificant as losing a shoe. Dad made God's presence a part of this situation, and how soothing that was, especially to Eliz.

Another example of Dad's sentimentality concerned the birth of our second child, our son Clifford. When Cliff was born, my parents happened to be staying at the Greenbrier Hotel in White Sulphur Springs, West Virginia. This is the hotel that Dad once joked about with the following story. He asked a bellhop for change for a dollar and was informed, "Sir, at the Greenbrier, a dollar is change!" Clifford was born at 1:11 a.m. on September 4, 1965, and at that early hour, I called the Greenbrier and asked for my parents' room. I got a hotel operator who informed me that these special people were not to be disturbed by any phone call. "Lady," I said, "I am their son, John, and my wife has just given birth to a son, and my parents will want to know about this no matter what time it is." Grudgingly, she put me through, and I gave my parents the happy news. Sleepy as they were, they were very glad and celebrated with me, asking many questions. Later, they wrote to us that, after the phone call, they got right down on their hands and knees and prayed for Cliff. They weren't being important this time; they were simply showing how much Cliff's birth meant to them. They were so happy that we had named him after Dad's father, Charles Clifford Peale. Their hearts swelled with pride and love.

Later in life, both in good times and bad, such sentimentality came to the fore in me. Even today, I still have the pair of red sneaker-like shoes that were the first shoes of our first child, Laura, now forty-nine years old. They are hung by my desk or in a drawer of my desk or by my bed—somewhere I see them often, always drawing love in my heart for my little baby girl. When we told Laura about these shoes, she rolled her eyes upward, as if to say, "There goes Dad again." But she always laughs happily. Except for pictures, we are not aware that Dad kept any such mementoes of us three kids.

Chapter 5: Becoming in My Enthusiasm for Sports

M y father was *not* a sportsman, although he was a sports fan—well, sort of, and when he had the time. As a boy, I did play golf with him, but only occasionally. I never engaged in that time-honored father-son activity of throwing a baseball back and forth. However, it is possible for me to say that he was an influence on my interest in and love for sports. This love has been an important lifelong factor in my becoming.

It started with baseball. My sister Maggie, almost three years my senior, remembers an important early incident regarding baseball. It was 1946, the last game of the pennant race in the National League between the Brooklyn Dodgers and the Saint Louis Cardinals. There was a final game of a three-game play-off series to decide the pennant race that was held at Ebbets Field in Brooklyn. Maggie remembers that Dad went to the principal of the Friends Seminary School in Manhattan where we both were students. He asked Mr. Alexander Prince for permission for us to miss school one day so that we could go see this game. Mr. Prince, as befitted his position as a school principal, was not in favor of this, but Dad argued that seeing the game would contribute to our education. In the end, the principal gave in and gave us permission.

So Dad took me and Maggie to the ball game. Although I don't exactly remember it, I suppose that our mother stayed home with our younger sister, Elizabeth, who at that time was only four years old. I was ten years old, and Maggie was twelve, soon to be thirteen.

I will never forget that game, nor will Maggie. We three had fun together, especially in the dramatic ending. In the ninth inning, the Cardinals were ahead by four runs, with the score eight to four. Harry "The Cat" Brecheen was pitching very well, Enos "Country" Slaughter was roaming the outfield, and Stan "The Man" Musial was playing first base. The Cardinals were a very good team. I believe that Burt Shotton was the manager of the Dodgers. I can't remember the lineup exactly, but at bat was a tall, lanky first baseman named Howie Schultz, who came to the plate with two outs in the ninth inning and the bases loaded. I dreamed that Schultz would hit a high drive for a grand-slam homerun, thereby tying the game for the Dodgers.

The fans were screaming encouragement, and Gladys Gooding played an encouraging song on the Ebbets Field organ. I could imagine how excited Red Barber was in the radio broadcast booth. With a full count, Brecheen pitched a fast ball, and "mighty" Howie Schultz struck out. Thirty-five thousand fans, a capacity crowd in Ebbets Field back then, heaved in unison a collective sigh of frustration. People were saying as we left, "Wait until next year." That was to be an exciting year with the coming of Jackie Robinson in 1947. I remember all this very clearly—how excited I was and then how disappointed I was with the ending. Maggie and I felt close to Dad that day.

We two kids and our relaxed father had a great time. He ordered us popcorn and soda pop from vendors in the stands. We ate hotdogs. I dreamt about catching a foul ball and had brought my glove in anticipation of that exciting possibility. Maggie and I jumped up and down, booing and cheering as our team had its ups and downs. I screamed in delight when Carl Furillo in right field threw a one-bounced beauty to the Dodger third baseman, who was able to tag a runner out that was trying to stretch a double into a triple. Our dad shared in many of our excitements, though he stayed in his seat much more than we did. We didn't see ourselves out with a man who was a minister and whose fame was on the increase; we saw ourselves with our loving father.

Then there was golf. Several times I played golf with Dad, often with Mother walking along with us for encouragement and exercise. I remember two specific golf events. The first was when we were on the fifth hole of the course at the Quaker Hill Country Club. I was on the fairway, looking to a shot for the green quite a distance away, but disturbed by the ugly wide ditch down the fairway between me and the flag on the green. I got visibly nervous and upset. My mother, in her accustomed way, tried to calm me down, singing her favorite song, "Let Me Call You Sweetheart," right on the golf course. It must have worked, for I hit a good high fairway wood over the ditch, landing in an easy pitching position for the green.

There was another special time on the golf course with Dad. Our twosome, with Mother again as a third party, was waiting to tee off on the first hole of the Quaker Hill course. Ahead of us was a foursome, including former governor of New York, Thomas E. Dewey, a neighbor on Quaker Hill. We decided that I could go ahead and drive, and I uncorked a beauty—a long, high drive that seemed to be headed right for the foursome. I was thirteen at the time, with a minister father and a mother who was a minister's daughter. Without thinking, I said, "Holy shit! I think my ball is going to hit the governor."

After this display of foul language, no attention at all was paid to the shot, which incidentally did not hit Governor Dewey. My parents were highly displeased with my verbal behavior. As I recall, I was forced to make a hasty exit off the golf course. We went home in silence, and I knew I was in trouble. This was confirmed by the lecture I received about my choice of words. I had plenty of time to realize what I had done, as I was sent to my room. Secretly, but with no specific evidence, I got the idea that my dad enjoyed the whole incident. However, in his position, he wasn't going to let me know that, even if it was true. As a parent, he took the stance of a disciplinarian. Yet, as someone who probably did the same sort of thing with his parents, he seemed to share my frustration, even to say what I had said.

I received encouragement from my parents in my earliest sports enthusiasms. Later, I was to become a true sports fan—and not just when I had time, like Dad. My first major sport was tennis, and I achieved some success, as I was a member of the varsity teams in both high school and college. I developed some good tennis skills, most notably a smooth drop shot and an "American twist," a spinning and high-bouncing service to the right. Once when I was playing in a competitive match, I stroked a beauty of an American twist serve, which fooled my opponent. It hopped from his forehand side to the backhand with a high bounce, which put him in a state of confusion. Instinctively, he raised his hand to catch the ball. All I needed to say was "nice catch."

I played endless sets of tennis during my high school and college years, notably with my still good friend Kim Wood. I won my fair share of tennis matches, with some great satisfaction. I carried my tennis racquet around, not to show off—or then again, maybe I did intend to show off my prowess.

With tennis, I passed beyond my parents' influence and interest. I did get some encouragement from them, but not much, as they were getting busy with work and becoming famous and influential. I refer here to an incident that occurred in 1955 in Burgenstock, Switzerland, where we were enjoying a summer vacation. During this time, my dad met with Billy Graham for a three-hour discussion about the up-and-coming Billy Graham Crusade to come to New York City in the fall. Dad was the minister of an important Fifth Avenue church, called Marble Collegiate Church, and Billy was trying to get support from him and other ministers in order for his crusade to be a success. Mother was also very much involved in these discussions.

At that time and place—I remember this with some emotional pain—I was playing tennis with my parents watching. I was playing well, and I knew it. I guess that I was trying to impress them. I was always trying to impress them with something or other—always wanting them to notice me and think well of me. On this occasion, after I finished playing, my mother, who had developed a serious critical streak, made negative remarks about my playing strategies. I cannot remember now exactly what she said back then, but I do remember the critical look on her face, which we three kids used to refer to as "the hard look."

I thought, *What is going on here?* I left her presence, thinking to myself that she really didn't know what she was talking about. They had noticed my tennis playing, but their reaction was critical—not approving. This was not a happy moment. I had impressed her all right, but it was in an undesirable way!

Over the years, my sisters and I experienced Mother's strong critical bent toward us. It is frustrating to seek approval and to get negative criticism instead. She could be that way with each of us. I don't remember her being that way with Dad, however. I think she knew that if she gave Dad "the hard look," he would perhaps have sunk down into the depths. I don't know if she ever knew the depressing effects of such behavior with us.

My sports enthusiasms developed significantly afterward and beyond parental influence. These interests have been a creative and exciting part of my becoming. I have been a strong tennis fan all my life, following some of my favorite tennis players through the years.

On the men's side, these players certainly include Poncho Gonzales and Roger Federer, and on the women's side, Chris Evert and Martina Navratilova. Every year, for as long as I can remember, I have watched many important matches in their entirety. So many long and exciting matches have come in all the four "majors" in Australia in January, in Paris Rolland Garros in May, in Wimbledon in July, and in the US Open in September. And all these years, I played tennis with pleasure and some success, as long as my left knee held out.

While in graduate school for my PhD at the University of North Carolina in Chapel Hill, I became a basketball fan of the Tar Heels. We followed the Heels closely, beginning with the end of the 1968–69 season in their tournament play. Similarly, I was excited when in 1982 with eighteen seconds to go in the game, Michael Jordan hit his outside jumper, which made "string music" as it swished through the net, to provide the go-ahead points over Georgetown in the finals of the same NCAA tournament, popularly called the "Big Dance" of 1982. I was pumped up once when Tar Heel guard Dudley Bradley, referred to by Carolina fans as "the secretary of defense," stole the ball from NC State's "Clyde the Glide" and again scored the game-winning basket. I loved when shooting guard Wayne Ellington scored several times from the outside in the NCAA Championship game against Michigan State in 2005, loosening up the inside so that Ty Lawson could practice his magic feeds to Tyler Hansbrough on the inside near the basket. UNC beat Michigan State, again winning the National Championship game.

As far as I know, my parents never had any interest in basketball or the Tar Heels. There was one occasion, however, when Dad told me about the entire Tar Heel team, together with Coach Dean Smith, coming to his church, the Marble Collegiate Church in New York City. I really didn't get the sense, however, that it was special to Dad because it was special for me. But he told about me about it the same way he might have told me about any group coming to his church.

With coaches Dean Smith and currently Roy Williams, there has been so much to be proud about and to cheer about as a Tar Heel fan. At the time of this writing, the Tar Heels are at the beginning of the 2011–2012 basketball season. They began the season ranked number one. Of course, any good basketball fan will think it far better for them to be ranked as such when the season approaches its climax in the NCAA tournament at the culmination of March Madness.

For thirteen years, from 1978 to 1991, I exercised myself in another sport, that of running. During those thirteen years, I ran over 1,000 miles per year. This was when we were living in Farmville, where I taught at Longwood College. There was a group of us, known as FARR —Farmville Area Road Runners—who ran together much of the time. Usually, however, I would leave the house, appear to be working to push down our large oak tree in our front yard while stretching my legs, and then take off by myself for runs of varying lengths. There was a particularly favorite route of mine along Germantown Road to Route 15, and then back a distance of about nine miles. This was a regular route for me. Sometimes I added more miles, and other times, I took a shortcut home. Once I met a curious boy who asked me where I was running to so fast. I said that I was running around in a huge circle. He asked, "What are you doing that for?"

He did not understand the joy of running—heading into the country in early morning mists or in the cool of the late afternoon summer's day, or running in crisp fall weather or even in the dead of winter when I sometimes would come home with icicles in my beard. He did not understand that after forty-five minutes of such extended physical exercise, the chemical basis of happy feelings is released from the base of the brain. He did not understand the chapter on "Running and Being" in a book by the famous runner Jim Fixx. I read an article once about a runner, written by his wife, who wrote, "My husband used to be a Methodist; now he is a runner."

There were road races around Virginia, our own "minithon," a 10K run of 6.2 miles from Hampden-Sydney College to Longwood College. Once I distinguished myself by running this course at a pace of under seven minutes per mile. I was at a peak in my physical condition at that time. There was also the Lynchburg Virginia 10-miler with a long uphill finish that broke the spirits of many a runner. And then in the early 1980s, I ran a marathon in Richmond. I came up the mile-long upgrade by the Country Club of Virginia at about nineteen or twenty miles into the run, "hitting the wall." I made it up over the hill, cruised into Shockoe Slip, and crossed the finish line, completing it in under four hours. These running years helped make my life happy and fulfilled.

Just after that race, I wrote my dad a letter saying how at the end of that great run, my mind was mush, my body hurt all over, but my spirits were soaring to the heights. What an exhilarating experience, replicating in my mind that first run from the Plains of Marathon to the City of Athens where the first marathon runner, Pheidippides, died as he uttered the word *nenikekamen*, translated from the Greek as "we have won" [the battle] to his fellow Athenians. Dad made much of this letter, actually reading it at the pulpit of Marble Church. He used it as a dramatic illustration of stamina and endurance. I believe that my dad was proud of me that day; at the least he had himself a good illustration for his sermon.

In the end, I still return to watching baseball, including the 2011 World Series between the St. Louis Cardinals and the Texas Rangers. It is like something from way back, which meant so much to me, draws me back to baseball. Enos Slaughter is no longer roaming in left field, and Stan "The Man" Musial is no longer playing first base, but I am still drawn to the Cardinals, who beat the Brooklyn Dodgers in 1946. Unlike my Dad, I did play catch with my son Cliff, and am, with him and his family, a current fan of the Cincinnati Reds. It does not escape me that my dad, who lived in Cincinnati during his high school years, was also a fan of what later became "the Big Red Machine."

Chapter 6: Becoming in Finding My Own Way

I t was not until late in my high school and early college days that I perceived *the deep and disturbing tension in my soul* between the influence of my dad and what I wanted to be, between trying to find my own way and living with a feeling that I also wanted to follow Dad and be close to him. Was I to follow in my father's footsteps or was I to launch out on my own? How would I become what I wanted to be, and in what direction would that take me? How would I be able to go on, sensing a separation from him and hurting because of that, and yet having the tenacity to follow my way for myself?

What complicated this was that I was feeling the negative impact of all this psychological confusion on my development. For me, these were disturbing and yet fundamental questions about my life and well-being. Naturally, through all of this, the sway of my love for and pride in my famous father was strong, but it grew increasingly negative and problematic.

In 1952, when I was in the middle of my high school years, *The Power of Positive Thinking* was published. With the hugely popular reaction to this book, something had changed; my dad became even more famous. Before the publication of his most celebrated book, Dad was well-known to a lesser extent as a public speaker at business conventions and meetings of various kinds. He had developed a large network of associates who supported him in his work with the new magazine called *Guideposts*, and the organization Mother started, called

31

The Foundation for Christian Living, later renamed the Peale Center for Christian living.

Here's how I perceive this increasing fame affecting my life. Earlier, before my high school years, there was a pattern to which my two sisters and I had to adjust. Dad would leave on Monday for speaking engagements all around the United States, taking his message of positive thinking out to business conventions and conferences and public meetings. This began to increase his fame, I suppose, but that was not my concern. Back he would come on Friday, only to closet himself in his study for the weekend in preparation for the Sunday services and sermon. It seemed abundantly clear that the *only* important thing that was happening in our family apartment in New York concerned what he was doing.

In a sense, Mother was a more difficult case for me than my dad. There has been much anger toward Mother over the years from me and, I believe, from my two sisters, Maggie and Eliz. My main reason is that Mother stood as the gatekeeper for my father, through which we children would have to enter to gain access to him. I recall one dismal night before high school when I actually asked my mother if I could speak to my father. *What is going on here?* I asked myself. I was like my uncle Bob, Dad's brother and two years his junior. When Bob saw that he had to go through his brother's wife to get to his brother, he got angry. He had the luxury of letting that be known. I felt that I had no such option. The frustration went inward in me, not outward at him.

I was fourteen when I actually asked my mother if I could speak to my father. She went to their back bedroom in our 1030 Fifth Avenue apartment to get Dad, and he returned securing the tie string on his bathrobe. Dad asked me in an abrupt way what I wanted to talk about. I was put off by his manner. Besides, it wasn't that I wanted to talk about anything specific. I had sensed that there was some distance growing between us. *What I really wanted was to connect personally with him.* I could see that it was not going to happen that night. I said something full of pathos: "Oh, nothing really." That was the end of that. Dad went back to get behind his screen and his gatekeeper in the privacy of their bedroom.

I'm not sure that my sisters sensed this gatekeeper role as much as I did. Maggie, the oldest, was the wisest. I see her as being able to be more open with her feelings about our parents. I believe she would have told Mother that she just wanted to have a connect time with Dad;

she would have insisted on it. With Elizabeth, the youngest, things got most difficult later on. Years later when Mother was the CEO of the Foundation for Christian Living—Mother also acted like a CEO with us three children—Elizabeth found herself in the position of being groomed for that spot. She was honored by that, and she worked hard to succeed in it. She was angered by Mother's behavior of making decisions without consulting with her or changing decisions they had made together without letting her know.

There were several times over the years when we would be talking over the telephone or together in person, and one of us would dissolve in tears in reaction to the ways of our mother. We three suffered together. We consoled and counseled with each other. As the years went by, this shared hurting helped bring us together. One of the richest blessings of my life has become the way we three are so very close. We are different in many ways, but we have an unshakable bond of love and sharing that is such a comfort to each of us.

Mother was often away from me and my sisters. She was away attending board meetings; by doing so, she felt she could contribute to and support her husband's career. Many of the boards were of important church organizations. We children were left in the hands of the maid, Alice Brown, from Jamaica, and sometimes her husband, Henry, a great guy. I attempted to make light of this situation, for I was quoted early on as saying that my mother worked at a lumberyard, for she went to so many board meetings!

My sisters and I were left to our own devices, and a deep impression grew in me that *what I was and what I was doing didn't matter.* I guess it was perceived that I was only a boy. But I was also developing personally, becoming a sensitive and independent-minded person. Perhaps I was taking after my parents in feeling this way, for they were independent-minded and sensitive also. It continued to seem, however, that nothing in our family was important except for the work that Dad was doing. For years, I lived with this tension in my soul, which deepened into a general sense that I wasn't worth much of anything at all. Looking back, it seems that there was a lack of parental encouragement.

My sister Maggie notes that they did come to her basketball games and pageants, and they encouraged her to buy new things. I remember only one time that my parents came to something for me—the senior play at my high school. Generally, I found that our parents were too highly focused on their own work. Perhaps my feelings about all of this remained below the level of consciousness in pre–high school days, but I did come to feel this strongly later in life.

To be sure, there are numerous positive memories that take me back to grade school years when my sisters and I were at the Friends Seminary School. And, of course, there were good memories amid the downside I now describe. One time, Dad came home from one of his trips, on this occasion from Chicago. He brought with him some dinner plates he had bought, with the remarkable claim that they were shatterproof. He said if he were to drop one on the hardwood floor, it would not break. We kids challenged him. I recall Mother looking like trouble was brewing. Dad threw a plate gently upward in a spiral motion. It fell on the floor and shattered into pieces, this to our happy amusement. Perhaps Dad set up the whole thing for family fun. At any rate, we all helped in the cleanup.

When high school years came along, I was away much of the time at Deerfield Academy, a prestigious prep school in Massachusetts, having a great time with my friends in our dorm, in class with our teachers, and out on the field playing tennis and running around the Potcumtuck Valley. I often worked out my stress on the cross-country running course in the valley, taking long runs along the Deerfield River.

When I got to college, the good life continued with me not having my classes at the top of my personal agenda, though I was impressed with the quality of my professors and their courses. I kept running and came in third in the Turkey Trot in November of my freshman year. I started dating girls in nearby colleges and playing tennis endlessly. I studied only when I felt I had to do so.

Then I woke up academically. At the end of my sophomore year, something good and important happened to me. As I was studying for an exam in a course called Introduction to Philosophy, with Professor Edwin Myers, I discovered that I had four days to study for that one final exam. I burned the midnight oil in McCormick Library at Washington and Lee to prepare, to study, to think, and to ponder my subject matter. In this process, I had the exhilarating feeling that I was onto something exciting. I found that I was getting somewhere, particularly in the understanding that I was developing.

Best of all, I found that I was really enjoying something by myself and for myself. My A grade on that examination confirmed my feelings that philosophy was something for me to pursue. I asked myself what could be wrong with being a philosophy major in college. What could be wrong in pursuing later a PhD in philosophy, with the dream of someday becoming a professor of philosophy? What could be wrong with seeking to become a Dr. Myers in my own life and work?

To my deep discouragement, it later became abundantly clear that there was something very wrong with all of this. There was something wrong with this for my dad. I was focusing on academics, the one area about which he was most sensitive. His inferiority complex kicked in most in academic settings. All through his education and his ministerial career, he felt inadequate in the intellectual side of life and especially sensitive when he received scathing criticism from the professor-types and theologians and churchman. During these years with Dad, I was rarely able to talk with him about philosophy or theology or anything important to me. When we did so, it never felt right to me; our personal disconnection was so readily apparent. I felt that he was putting me down. I felt that my chosen endeavor had never been accepted. I was never encouraged in my sometimes tentatively expressed views, which I was seeking to clarify and develop.

I sensed, however tentatively at this time, that there was a deterioration of my relation with my dad. I wondered if he was threatened by my intellect or by my deep interest in intellectual life. I questioned whether he was so insecure and self-absorbed that he really didn't care what I had to say. What did he think about me as a son?

Clearly, the disconnect with my father was starting to lay the foundation for trouble ahead. Did I sense all of this at that time in my life? Or was I oblivious to what was happening in my soul at the time? Maybe he just took me as a troubled college student.

As we were growing up, my two sisters and I sought approval from our parents. For me, it was in relation to my dad, and for my sisters, it was, perhaps, more so with our mother. One thing perfectly clear was that each of us was seeking basically the same thing. I never felt satisfied in this as a young person and also later in life.

As children, something happened to us as a result of the parenting we received. I didn't realize the negative effect of this right away. I recall one time, much later in life, when I got angry with Lydia's sister, Ann, in a public family setting. It was an unhappy time, as I was ashamed by the display of my anger, and my family was not happy with the way I acted. After the dust settled, Maggie and I had a talk. In her first sentence, she said something revealing to me: "What did our parents do to us?"

Due to my emotional upset at the time, I did not ask what Maggie meant. I think she was questioning the effect of our parents on us from the time we were young, seeing all the problems arising in me as I continued to seek approval. Maggie was communicating the fact that all this had troubling effects on us, and that it might have been a factor in the emotional way I reacted at the time.

After my high school years, I lost something so personal and meaningful to me that, up until lately, it had been hard for me to think about or talk about. I felt then, and I feel now, that *I lost the close, personal contact I had with my dad* in pre–high school days. I am not sure when such a realization came fully into my conscious mind. Perhaps I only realized the full implications of this loss when I was in graduate school and during my early career as a professor of philosophy. But lose this personal connection I did, or I felt strongly that I did. And it really hurt and made me deeply frustrated.

This loss was something that became more and more onerous as my life developed. I felt the need to try to get it back, in ways that were difficult, frustrating, and apparently futile. I never succeeded in that effort. It became such an important factor in the generation of anger and later a depression that, in my late fifties and early sixties, took me down to the depths of despair.

As I look back from the perspective of my life today, I have come to understand how I tried to get back the close personal contact that I no longer felt but wanted so much. I can see how I tried to do this in many ways, some subtle, and all demeaning, frustrating, and futile.

Most notably, I tried to get it back by making important speeches to show Dad what I thought of him and how I loved and respected him and how much I wanted his love and respect toward me. There were two major speeches I made with this objective in mind. These speeches were made in Dad's presence.

The first came at an important anniversary of Dad at Marble, that of the twenty-fifth year in early October 1957, when I was a junior in college. I have no record of what I said on this occasion, only the memory of feeling that in spite of my efforts, nothing really changed. It was like he and I were just going through the motions of saying what should be said on such an anniversary. This hurt me. I had clear awareness of continued distance from Dad. I had a deep frustration and a sense of emptiness. How was I ever to succeed in capturing what I had lost? I kept on trying to bridge the gap between us, but my efforts were in vain.

The second such speech was on the occasion of Dad's fortieth anniversary at Marble Collegiate Church. In this talk, I praised him openly, and he responded generously. Yet I still felt that we hadn't really connected. Again I said what I believed I should have said. Again he responded as he should have responded. But in the end, something was still missing. Again I was hurt. I asked myself whether he had any idea of the hurt I was experiencing. It came to me that he probably didn't have a clue about how I was feeling deep down. I didn't like that answer. Yet I kept trying to bridge the disconnect that separated us.

An opportunity came along for a final speech—at his memorial service, or as it is now called, a "celebration-of-the-life-of" service for someone who has passed away. Of course I knew that I couldn't really connect with him at that service. Maybe I was trying somehow to make my final peace with him. It was clear that I was making an effort to present him and the way I felt about him to the world, to the large number of people in attendance. I told myself that I would make a final effort, in which I would compose and present a very well-prepared speech, something that Dad valued so much.

I decided that I would praise him to the skies with eloquence, a speech that people would hopefully long remember. I also decided that I would be like him in the delivery—that is, I would stand at the pulpit without notes, with no podium between me and the congregation. Like he did, I would be the whole man speaking to those who loved him as he had spoken to them. I did as I had planned in what was a final but ultimately futile effort to recover what was lost. With the finality of Dad's passing on, the finality of the disconnection hit home. This hurt me yet again.

Interlude 1:
Two Efforts to Bridge the Gap between Me and My Dad

⌒ψ⌒⌐

1. The Fortieth Anniversary Service of Norman Vincent Peale at the Marble Collegiate Church, New York City, December 1, 1972.

Report of the Service and Speech

No personal records of this occasion remain with me, and this report comes from the Pawling-Patterson (New York) *News-Chronicle*, dated Thursday, October 5, 1972. I have a clear memory of having had this newspaper before. The main headline reads: "Son Pays Tribute to Dr. Peale for 40 Years at Marble Church." A subheadline reads: "President Nixon Sends Congratulations."

It is reported in the newspaper that I was speaking for my sisters, Margaret and Elizabeth, something I never intended to do. It is also reported that Dr. Peale baptized his eighth grandchild, Andrew Peale Allen, son of his daughter Elizabeth and her husband, John Allen, a senior editor of *Reader's Digest*.

It was noted that Mother, who had occupied the same seat in the same pew, was given forty red roses.

I said that it meant a great deal to me to be standing at that pulpit that day. I spoke of Dad's long, varied, and outstanding ministry there, in which he had opened himself up to his congregation. I noted that in this special service, we were not only recognizing the man but also the message, and the team ministry of my father and my mother. Dad and Mother were in fact one complex personality, and we received much of him through her.

On behalf of the family, I told my dad that we honored him on this, his fortieth anniversary celebration at Marble. I said straight out that we wished him and Mother the very best in the rest of their lives. I even said that they had given us a gift, none less than the very faith and character and the abundant riches of their very lives. "Whatever we have attained, whatever character we have developed, has come to us as a direct result of guidance from you and Mother."

My dad said he was moved by my remarks, putting it mildly. He noted that it meant a great deal to him that I would even think of saying these things. "I assure you there has never been any generation gap between the two of us. I love him very much and am so terribly proud of him—for having made speeches all my life and listened to them—to be able to stand up here in these circumstances and make a speech so felicitous, despite the subject matter, is truly remarkable. It was a gem, in expression and thought and in feeling. I tell you, John, I'll remember it all my life."

Dad glanced down to the pew where Mother sat and added, "Anything I have done could never have been done without her. So as long as I can see her dear face down there in the pew, I'll be happy."

Rev. Arthur Caliandro read a congratulatory letter from President Nixon, expressing the hope that "the service will bring you as much satisfaction as you have brought to others." The statement from Nixon went on to send prayers and warmest wishes from the entire Nixon family. He noted that my dad had substantially fortified the moral fiber of America and strengthened the future of our society. Mr. Nixon concluded by noting that Mr. and Mrs. Nixon had attended Marble Church, and their daughter, Julie, and David Eisenhower were married there.

Aftermath of the Service and Speech for Me

At the time, it meant quite a good deal to me to contribute to this celebrative occasion as I did. I was quite nervous but acquitted myself well enough, I thought. Dad and others told me so. As I look back now, it seems that my reaction had two levels. I was pleased about the praise from Dad and the outright expression of love and respect from him. I felt good that he said he loved me, and I realized how genuine an expression that was for him.

But there was another level, in which I felt the difficulties of such loving expressions, as I was beginning at that time to more clearly realize in my conscious mind the separation that had come between us, that I had lost a close personal contact with him, and that this effort to get it back was being fulfilled on a superficial level only, lacking something deep. I realized that both Dad and I were saying what was appropriate to our stations in life on such an anniversary occasion. We both said it well, and the newspaper picked up on a theme so appreciated by fans of NVP—that is "Son Pays Tribute." This is what people like to hear, and it is what they like to experience in their own lives with their fathers. Yet I felt that I was left right where I was. In fact, I was left there for the next thirty plus years—until I came into the Sunlight of the Spirit in my recovery in my seventies.

2. The "Celebration of the Life of Norman Vincent Peale" at the Marble Collegiate Church, New York City, December 29, 1993.

The Setting for the Service and Speech

Together with Rev. Arthur Caliandro, Minister of Marble Collegiate Church, the family decided that there would be four talks by family members during the service—first Margaret, then me, then Elizabeth, and then Mother. The service was to be a full worship service with a sermon, hymns, choir, family talks, and the playing and singing of Handel's "Hallelujah Chorus" at the end. There was a closed casket in the front of the church, just below the raised platform that was the pulpit.

I worked hard at the composition of the speech that I was to make. It was unusual, however, that in my preparation, I wrote nothing down on paper. Between our mother and us three children, we had agreed only on time that each of us would have about seven minutes. Maggie's talk was first, since she was the oldest, and Elizabeth, as the youngest, came third. Each of them delivered fine tributes in their own distinctive ways. I decided that I would tell about my dad, presenting him as I knew and felt about him. I also decided that I would preach like he did at the Marble pulpit—without notes or a lectern in front of me. So I composed the speech in outline, writing down nothing and going over it enough, I hoped, to be ready when the time came to make it. For me, this was a challenging, even a scary matter.

The Speech

" My dad was reared by Charles Clifford Peale and Anna Delaney Peale, his parents, in small towns and villages in an area he loved to call southern Ohio, the heartland of America.

"In 1910 in that same area, the family gathered together—Dad was twelve then—to enjoy the splendors of the passing of Halley's Comet. An important conversation took place. 'Do you think that I will ever live to see Halley's Comet come again?' asked Dad. And Clifford Peale in his typical fashion said, 'That is not the question, Norman. The important question is what you will make of yourself in the interim.'

"Now Dad did live to see Halley's Comet come again, and then some. What I want to say to you today is what he did indeed make of himself.

"It seems that life for Norman Peale started slowly, as he was a shy, retiring, thin young man, with a large inferiority complex. But he managed to get himself educated and prepared for the ministry and came after a while to the University Methodist Church in Syracuse, New York. And there he met Ruth Stafford, and they were married, and he made of himself a husband. And Mother and Dad lived together, happily, creatively, and productively for over sixty-three years. Along the way, they bore and reared us three children, whom you see before you now.

"And then he came here and was senior minister of this church for fifty-two years. And he got hold of the idea of positive thinking and the power this idea had, enabled by God's grace and the presence of the Lord Jesus Christ, to change human life and to help people live better, including himself.

"And he made of himself on this pulpit a preacher. Art Caliandro knows, as do I, how powerful he was as a preacher. And Margaret and Elizabeth and I would watch him from the pastor's pew down there, as he stood here, as I am endeavoring to do now without notes, without a lectern between him, the whole man, and the people he loved.

"And he preached with power. We watched him with admiration and love in our hearts as he inspired us, as he made us laugh, as he made us cry, until he had us right where he wanted us, and then we were really ready to hear his message, and he preached that to us, the timing designed for maximum good for the audience.

"This is called the art of oratory, and he was a master of the art. While here he made of himself a counselor with his down-home native rapport and love of people, and together with the eminent psychiatrist Smiley Blanton, he started a religio-psychiatric clinic, which still provides excellent counseling services at a relatively low cost to troubled people in this city.

"And as I like to think about it, he went out from this, his spiritual home, to take his ministry to people everywhere. He became a radio personality through the richness of his voice, and a TV personality, which programming was considerably beautified by the presence of my mother on the program with him.

"As we all know he became a platform speaker in the secular area, of great power and success in all sorts of conventions and public meetings.

"And he became an author of many good books, bought by millions, and read by them, and helped by the books they read.

"And Mother, the organizational genius, and Dad, the creative genius, joined together as a team and made of themselves magazine writers, editors, and publishers, and they started two organizations that published magazine articles and different kinds of literature and sponsored different kinds of activities and conferences. I'm talking about Guideposts and Sermon Publications Inc., now the Peale Center for Christian Living. It is a testimony to the effective leadership of my parents that the organizations on the back of your programs are all creative, vital, healthy organizations, well-funded economically with talented and dedicated staffs that are well positioned and eager and ready to carry the message of positive thinking into the future.

"Along the way, this country boy from Bowersville, Ohio, and this country girl from Fonda, Iowa, became famous. This is illustrated in the family talk by the account Mother gives—if I remember this correctly—of their attendance at an affair at the Nixon Library in California some years ago, when four gentleman came up to my parents and said, "Hi, Norman. Hi, Ruth." The names of these people were George H. W. Bush, Ronald Reagan, Gerald Ford, and Richard Nixon. If Mr. Jimmy Carter had been there, I'm sure he would have spoken similarly.

"And he became highly influential over the course of his life. You should see the letters that came in that testify to the influence that this man had in the writers' lives for their own good.

"What we in our family are most proud of is the way he was loved. My dad gave of himself to try to help people live better lives, and in the course of this, he genuinely loved them. People knew it and loved him in return.

"So in summary, Clifford Peale's question of 1910 can be answered in the following way: my dad made of himself and became one of the most important and beloved religious leaders ever produced in the United States of America. That's what my dad did.

"And now he is gone, and the loss is profound and the grief deep. We loved him in such a special way, and he loved us. And we Peales are going to have to learn to live with the loss and the grief.

"But there is one thing more. In our grief, in our loss, there is a peace—even a joy—that Dad has become reunited with Charles Clifford and Anna Delaney, and with Bob and Leonard and other loved ones in the light and love of our Heavenly Father and in the fellowship of Jesus Christ, his Lord and Savior.

"Just maybe, if I am worthy, and if we are worthy, and if it be God's will, there will come the day when we too will rejoin him in God's eternal presence."

The Aftermath of the Speech and the Service

I received much enthusiastic commendation for my speech and my part in the service. Many people complimented me on a job well done, and I could see admiration in their eyes. In the view of some people, I had produced a gem, capturing the sense of the man, with deep emotion yet subtle phraseology and eloquence, and as one person said, it took guts to stand up there like that under those circumstances.

I had stood at the pulpit looking at my two sisters and my wife, Lydia, for support and my three children, Laura, Clifford, and Lacy, not to mention my two brothers-in-law, Paul Everett and John Allen. Our wider family was congratulatory of what each of the three of us did in this unusual event. What struck me most, when I was saying the final sentence of spiritual hope in my talk, was my son, Cliff, wiping a tear out of his eye. For those who know this sometimes sarcastic man, such a reaction was distinctly unusual. I was touched by this show of feeling in this son of ours, who carries the name of one I respected so very much, his paternal great-grandfather, Charles Clifford Peale. I was happy to feel and have this connection with him.

I will never forget the reaction of Arthur Caliandro, a friend of mine and our family for at least forty years. He stood right in front of me and close, put his arms around my shoulders, looked me in the eye, and said, "John, this was your moment of greatness."

When opportunity presented itself after the service, I managed to have a moment to myself in the men's room, standing before the mirror and looking into my eyes, seeing pride and love, but also pain and emptiness. In a sense, I felt cheap and dishonest with myself. I had done what I did and was supposed to do, putting myself into it wholeheartedly and doing it well, but I still felt the deep anger and frustration that I had felt for years over losing contact with my father. And I took offense at the statement of Arthur Caliandro, even though I'm sure he meant well. Was "my moment of greatness" only when I was praising my dad? Had I ever had a moment of greatness for and by myself? I asked myself why I was in a position to ask myself that devaluing and demeaning question.

Chapter 7: Becoming in High School, College, and Graduate Studies

Deerfield Academy

My parents decided to send me away for high school to a prestigious boarding school: Deerfield Academy in Deerfield, Massachusetts. There was one event that led them, particularly my mother, to do this. While in seventh or eighth grade, I was taking piano lessons at Turtle Bay Music School, which was located on Fifty-Second Street off of Lexington Avenue. One day on my way home, I was quite careless when I came to Lexington Avenue and jaywalked out into the street. I was hit by a taxicab coming north and plumped down in a sitting position right in the middle of the traffic-filled street. I was stunned and crying, and my books and papers were strewn all around me.

Traffic stopped momentarily on that side of the street as I got up and collected my things. I didn't really think about any injury, although my upper left leg was sore and beginning to swell up. The taxi driver put me in his cab and took me home, coming with me up to our apartment on the eighth floor, standing with me at the door when it was opened by my shocked parents. He explained the situation, and Mother thanked and tipped him. Next, she put me in a hot bath with Epsom salts. Only then did I reflect on how dangerous what had occurred was. Even today, there is an area in my upper left leg that feels partially dead, and I believe it is a result of that accident. I was okay, though I would never forget the incident.

It was my mother who thought that it was a good idea to send me away to prep school where I would have plenty of room to run around safely. Most of my life, I have said to others, half-kiddingly, that I was sent away to get some character development. I was fourteen at the time. I was getting that at home, of course, although at that time in my life, I didn't give it much thought. What is apparent to me now is the character development I received in the various schools I attended, beginning with Deerfield. I learned from and was influenced personally very much by my influential teachers and the course content. Beginning at this special place with "the sons of Deerfield," schooling in the broader sense played a large role in making me what I have become today.

Deerfield was a great match for me, as I learned much and had good friends. My personality became more formed and developed there. Classes were good and challenging, and Deerfield was where I first felt the excitement of learning. I remember a course in Ancient History with Mr. Williams and the book we had, *Ancient Times: A History of the Early World*, by James Breasted. This became a famous book; it was Breasted who coined the phrase "the Fertile Crescent" to describe a way of imagining the whole Middle East region. Later in my travels in the Holy Land, such a mental capacity boded well for my spiritual development. It was Mr. Suitor, teacher of English, with whom I had that meaningful exchange in study hall when I was reading James Hilton's *Lost Horizons*. He was also the proctor in the Indian House where I made good friends, such as my roommate, Jim Stevens. Our dormitory was named Indian House to commemorate the Indian raid on the town of Deerfield in 1704. Life in the Indian House was lots of fun, and life there presented constant opportunities for diverting amusements to test the patience and character of Deerfield teachers and staff.

One such time of amusement for us young students occurred in a proctored study hall, a large room with many of us students present. We devised this clever plan to start humming together after the striking of the noon hour on the big school clock. The proctor, a new teacher just getting his feet wet dealing with the likes of us, told us to stop humming. Now it is difficult for a person to be able to tell among others who is and who is not humming. When the humming did not stop, he became angry and said that if we did not stop, he would keep us after school in the study hall. *Hummmm* went we. Then he increased the time we would have to stay after classes. *Hummmm* continued we. Finally, red-faced, he left the room, and we had him beat.

The next time we were in that study hall, an experienced teacher was our proctor. We started to hum after the noon striking of the school clock. He told us to stop. *Hummmm* went we. Then he picked out one of us, a boy named Bob Nichols, a good friend of mine. The teacher stood up, tall and straight, a big man with his hands hooked into his belt, and said, "Nichols, if you don't stop humming, I am going to come down to your seat and knock your teeth so far down your throat that you're going to have to open your fly to smile." We all started laughing. Now it is hard to hum and laugh at the same time. In the ongoing game that we students played with the teachers and staff, it was we who were beaten this time.

And then there were sports. It was at Deerfield that I began to run, under the influence of a good runner and friend, Jerry Murphy of the cross-country team. I took to it immediately and got a great sense of satisfaction running the 2.6-mile course. At Deerfield, I developed a good tennis game and had many successful and competitive matches in interscholastic competition, as well as keen competition with such fine tennis players as my fellow varsity team member Bob Cushman. Both the running and the tennis became lifelong loves. Another sport that I developed in was squash, and I was on the varsity team. In one match, I came back to win a best-of-five-games match. Our coach, Mr. Reid, told me something after the match that I still remember: "John, today you became a squash player." To me, it meant that I was becoming good at something I loved. That was the reinforcement I needed. It was good for me, a young boy, to know that I was good at something and recognized and appreciated for that talent. At home, I had not received much of this kind of recognition. At Deerfield, the idea was creeping into my consciousness that I really was worth something.

Singing in the Deerfield Glee Club under the direction of the faculty master, Ralph Oatley, was one of my major accomplishments at Deerfield. Mr. Oatley had a great impact on my life at Deerfield. I loved to listen to him talk, and I respected his conducting ability in dramatic understatement. I was especially proud of being one of the leads in our senior play, *The Pirates of Penzance,* an operetta by Gilbert and Sullivan. Later, my family made fun of me by kidding that the only reason I got the part was because I was the boy who had the most hair on his chest! I do remember that on the night of our performance, my parents seemed to be proud of me.

I was impressed that my parents, especially my dad, actually made the trip from New York to Deerfield, Massachusetts, to see me on this important occasion in my life. The year was 1954, two years after the publication of *The Power of Positive Thinking*. The fact that he came, busy as he was, was a sign that there might be hope that things could be changing for the better between us. This was when I was just beginning to get a sense of the gap between us. He seemed to approve of my performance. And that felt good.

I recall that my parents drove me to Deerfield on my initial trip there, and they stayed around for sentiment's sake, even sitting in the car outside Indian House, watching me and Jim Stevens getting ready for bed the first night in our front room, with curtains wide open.

A major attraction and asset of Deerfield was its headmaster, "The Head," named Frank L. Boyden, one of the great prep school leaders of our generation. I still recall, and my parents liked to tell the story of my interview with him, when he turned to a colleague with a nod, which meant that I had been admitted. It was an early Deerfield sign that I was becoming something worthwhile. That in itself was an important step in my personal development, my becoming. Mr. Boyden was a huge influence on us boys at Deerfield. I will never forget to my dying day the advice he gave us senior boys as we were sitting on the floor with legs crossed in the New Dorm front room. He told us the words of Philippians, a lesson for us to take with us for life: "Whatever is true, whatever is honorable, whatever is just, whatever is pure, whatever is lovely, whatever is gracious, if there is any excellence, if there is anything worthy of praise, think about these things. And the Peace of God, which passes all understanding, will keep your hearts and minds in Christ Jesus" (Phil. 4:8–9). The last sentence, which has meant so much to me throughout my life, was part of his farewell talk to the members of the class of 1954, and it was a proud moment for me and my classmates.

Washington and Lee University

When I graduated from Deerfield, most all my friends were going away to college in the Northeast, where I had spent the last four years. I wanted something different. My sister was at Ohio Wesleyan, from which Dad had graduated long ago. Somehow the idea came to me to go south, and I discovered Washington and Lee University, a fine school nestled in the hills of central Virginia. Something drew me to this beautiful place and to Virginia, where I have lived now for over forty years. Living, studying, and working in Virginia, starting with college, has been so stimulating and important to me in the process of my becoming.

By this time, I had developed an independent streak, yet another characteristic that boded well for my becoming. After I had looked into the college situation to my own satisfaction, I simply informed my parents that I was going to college at Washington and Lee University in Lexington, Virginia. I do not remember that they were involved in this decision at all; perhaps they were just too busy with their important work. They had not heard of the college I chose, and later they took a trip to Washington and Lee and met with the president, G. Pendleton Gaines, to ask why their son wanted to go to his college. They said that they had come to Lexington to see what it was like.

Two of my good friends, one of my tennis-playing friends, Kim Wood, and one of my glee club friends, Brad Gooch, had also decided to go to Washington and Lee, so the three of us headed south. These friendships were important factors in my decision. We three loved what we found—a beautiful place with an excellent faculty, an intelligent student body, and a good learning environment. The idea of learning struck me forcibly in an opening meeting of freshmen when Dean James G. Leyburn showed us his love of lifelong learning. At the end of his talk, he quoted the words on the tombstone of a man he admired: "He died learning." I came to think that those words would suit my marker as well. Lifelong learning has been such a rich component in my becoming.

As I noted in my section on becoming by trying to find my own way, I talked about not taking my studies seriously until the end of my sophomore year. Then I became a student and started down the road envisioned by Dean Leyburn. Sophomore year, I took Leyburn's Ancient History class and actually wept at his depiction of the death scene of Socrates as recounted in the *Phaedo* of Plato. The next year, I returned to that class to hear the same lecture, and I was sentimental once more. I had the experience of Dr. Leyburn's style of wisdom and character, and I was touched emotionally. At my first teaching post at Elmhurst College in Illinois, I could see some former students out in the hallway, listening attentively to my lectures, being sentimental, if not actually crying. This kind of influence and rapport with students has been important to me throughout my long teaching career, a significant mark of my becoming.

I took the courses of faculty I admired: Jenks in European history, Fishwick in art and culture, Jenkins in art of painting, Turner in American history, and Harvey Wheeler in political science and philosophy. For my first two years, my academic work was rather undistinguished. I guess the influence of such a good faculty took root slowly in my mind. I hadn't studied all that hard during my first two years. But then things began to change. In my junior year, I took Professor Harvey Wheeler's course, Political Philosophy, determined to get an A grade not only in his course, but A grades in all my courses my last two years. I had a B+ going into Wheeler's final exam. He posed an essay topic I felt sure I could not ace. So I was bold, suggesting another essay topic, a really good one, on which I wrote a brilliant essay. He called me into his office and said, "John, your essay topic was very good, and your essay was excellent, but I want you to know that I will pose the topics, and you will write on what I choose for you. He gave me a B+ grade. I was disappointed, but secretly I knew that I had succeeded.

I did well in college in leadership, sports, and, in my last two years, in my academic studies. As at Deerfield, I was gaining recognition and respect from others. As I said earlier in this book, my main inspiration was from Dr. Edwin Myers, professor of philosophy. He was such a good scholar and a demanding and challenging teacher, an impressive model of a faculty member. I found out that he would get up at 5:00 a.m. to do his serious work before the busyness of the day began. In my own teaching life, I followed the same helpful habit. My dad, who worked all the time, never quite had this schedule.

For me, Edwin Myers reflected the kind of day had by Immanuel Kant of Konigsberg, in East Prussia—now Kaliningrad in Russia, his hometown. Kant was the philosopher most admired by Myers, and it was years before I had the philosophical insight to see that Myers was wrong about some things about Kant or even that—God forbid—Kant himself was wrong!

But Kant has been a model philosopher for a whole century, especially in the mythology about his day. Like Myers, he too would rise early in the morning to write his philosophy, which brought to conclusion divergent paths in philosophy on the continent of Europe and on the British Isles. In the history of philosophy, it can be seen as a position that lasted for almost a hundred years! It was that long before people considered philosophy without taking into consideration what Kant had said!

After writing in the morning, he would go to his university and lecture—profess—what he had written, and then come home to have a sumptuous midday repast where people beat a pathway to his door to talk with him and to listen. Then he would take his walk for exercise. It is said that the town clock-keeper would set the clock in the church steeple by the regularity of Kant's walks. Then he would retire to his study for reading and contemplation in preparation for writing the next morning. It is said that after age fifty, Kant never read anyone except himself! He was perhaps the vainest of men, and if you're going to be vain, you had better be good, as was he.

I developed a personal goal—to be like Dr. Myers and like Kant in my academic work and in my college teaching. When I was teaching at Virginia Tech in the Governor's School for the Gifted in 1982, I visited another retired professor there named Marshall Fishwick, whom I had had as a teacher at Washington and Lee. On his office wall was a picture of Dr. Myers, with Arnold and Mrs. Toynbee, when Toynbee was visiting the campus in the spring of 1958. I told Dr. Fishwick that I wanted a copy of that picture. He obliged me. The photography clinic at the university took the picture out of the frame and copied it. I got it reframed, and it has hung on the wall of my study ever since.

Professor Myers had arranged for Professor Arnold Toynbee, author of the famed *A Study of History*, to spend the second semester of the 1957–58 academic year, my senior year, on our campus. My good friend Cliff Smith and I would pore over the material, working up profound questions we thought would be a challenge for him to answer. We would pose them to Professor Toynbee in our weekly seminar with him. While our questions seemed profound to us, we were taken aback by his humble responses. After suggesting the lines along which an answer could be formed, he turned the tables on us and asked us what we thought. We were not really prepared for that.

In my senior year at Washington and Lee, Mother and Dad took their second trip to Lexington. It had been a long time since their first visit, and I did not feel good about that. Again, I guess they were too busy with their own work and lives. On this second trip, Dad came to be an invited guest speaker at the same Lee Chapel at which Leyburn had spoken so well four years earlier. I was proud as I could be of my father, who made a rousing speech, very much appreciated by students and faculty alike—a grand occasion. My final days in Lexington were satisfactory, all the way through graduation in June 1958. I had already started becoming like Dr. Myers.

The influence of my father on the rest of my education was negligible. I was going in my own way more deeply into academics in my philosophical and theological studies, and as such, further away from his way, or so it was perceived by him. What I didn't know was that trouble was brewing for him; I had no disturbed feelings about that until the fall of 1960.

Boston University

I went to Boston University for a master's in philosophy, very much enjoying this famous city, seemingly the best of US cities for graduate students. I went to BU just as my dad had done, except my focus wasn't at the School of Theology, though I did take courses there. Like my dad, I discovered Boston Personalism in the Philosophy Department, and like him, I was put off by it. Personalism is a philosophy that was developed at BU by Borden Parker Bowne. In one sentence, it can be described as follows: the person is the basic category for explaining reality; only persons are real. Much more can be said, of course.

At BU, I did serious work in philosophy, including studying outstanding examples of nineteenth- and twentieth-century grand-scale metaphysics of major figures in the field. I refer to such works as F. H. Bradley's *Appearance and Reality*, Brand Blanshard's *The Nature of Thought*, and Samuel Alexander's *Space Time and Deity*. As noted above, I was absorbed by much of the work of William James. In addition, I studied Hinduism and Buddhism with Amiya Chakravarty, as well as writing a thesis on St. John of the Cross and Ramakrishna. Not to be forgotten were the courses on the history of philosophy, notably a Kant seminar on *The Critique of Pure Reason*. This deepening and sharpening of my philosophical acuity in reflections on these established scholars and writers was a significant step in my personal development. They became models and foil against which I began to develop my own mature philosophy.

In Boston, I fell in love with Lydia Daniel Woods. She and I had been friends in college. She had studied at Mary Baldwin College, in Staunton, Virginia, near Lexington. I was a student at Boston University, and across the Charles River, Lydia worked at Harvard University and entered the master's in teaching program there. Early in my time in

Boston, my BU roommate, Jim Jordan, and I went to a party given by Lydia and her housemates in Cambridge. On the way home, Jim told me that Lydia liked me!

Lydia and I dated and fell in love, and each of us began the process of disentangling from previous romantic involvements. During the process of our courtship across the river, Lydia took me to a park bench in Cambridge and told me what she actually thought of Norman Vincent Peale. She said that she had questions about whether the goal of life, especially the Christian life reflected in *The Power of Positive Thinking*—happiness or feeling good about one's self—was really the point. It was not that she opposed NVP's point of view so much as she needed to get these kinds of reservations off her mind. I was not bothered about this one bit, as I was coming to be able to handle people who had questions about my father's viewpoint.

Our relationship blossomed and grew until one night I called her up from a phone booth in a Walgreens drug store off Charles Street, at the base of Beacon Hill in Boston. I did not go to see her that night, for she was studying for an exam in her Harvard course on educational psychology with Professor George Goethals. Our telephone talk took an unexpected turn, and suddenly, I popped the question: "Will you marry me?" She said, "You don't have to ask me that." I allowed that I didn't *have* to ask her, but I was asking her anyway, and after a short hesitation, she said, "Yes." My heart leapt for joy, certain as I was that she was for me. She received a B+ on her exam, not her accustomed A grade.

An important experience for me in Boston was meeting Professor Paul Tillich from Harvard. I had been reading his *Systematic Theology* and found Friedrich Wilhelm Joseph von Schelling's *The Ages of the World* nestled philosophically beneath Tillich's viewpoint in the first volume of his *Systematic Theology*. I found Tillich's view stimulating and theologically fascinating and compelling. His influence seemed to be enormous. I deeply respected him and his work.

One day I was studying in Widener Library at Harvard, but before getting to work, I practiced the time-honored evasion of study by students: reading newspapers. On this occasion, I was stopped short as I read a scathing theological criticism by Professor Tillich of the viewpoints of both Norman Vincent Peale and Billy Graham. I got upset, for *I found myself caught between a man I respected for his thinking and my father, whom I loved.* My love was mixed with feelings of frustration and anger, in which I was caught as I was trying to find my own way in life. This was not a new position for me and not the last time I was squeezed into this kind of uncomfortable situation.

I wandered around Widener in a state of emotional confusion, until I found myself at the door of Professor Tillich's office. I knocked, and the door opened, and there was the great man etched in the doorway. I introduced myself. He invited me in and said, "Oh, I have said some unkind things about your father." We talked for almost an hour, and he was kind and understanding, opening up to me, a young man, telling about his German, dictatorial, rule-the-roost minister father whom he had to "learn to love in silence."

We connected! I was so impressed and appreciative of his human and caring response to my dilemma. We talked about Union Theological Seminary, where I was headed in the fall, and he spoke so well of that institution. I had been thinking of going into the ministry ever since I was in college, but I had not yet told my parents about my decision to go to Union Seminary. Professor Tillich and I talked of a trip he was taking to Japan, and I told him about living conditions there, as I had recently come back from a trip with my parents in 1957. It was a time that I will never forget. It helped me in my quest for finding my own way, to share that need with a man I so respected as Tillich. He had found his way in the professorial profession of theology. Why couldn't I do the same with my father? It gave me a feeling of support and made me more confident. In Boston, with metaphysics, the lure of the interesting city, falling in love with Lydia, and connecting with Paul Tillich, there was significant personal development going on in me.

I left Boston and my graduate studies there to go to New York and enter Union Theological Seminary in the fall of 1960. Unbeknownst to me at the time, this was to be a crucial and enormously difficult time for my dad and our family.

Chapter 8: Becoming at Union Theological Seminary; Trouble for Dad

⟨flourish⟩

In the fall of 1960, I entered Union Theological Seminary in Morningside Heights in New York City, just down the street from Columbia University. My entrance there was unexpectedly dramatic, for on that very day on the front page of the *New York Times*, there was a picture of my dad preaching and gesticulating in his usual oratorical way. This was accompanied by an article discussing Peale's participation in a group of conservative Christian ministers who had come together in Washington, DC, on September 7, 1960, to consider the potential problems should a Roman Catholic become president of the United States. John Fitzgerald Kennedy was a candidate for president that year. In the article was a quotation from John C. Bennett of the Union Seminary faculty, stating the opinion that "'the Peale group' had loosed the gates of the Protestant underworld."

In the previous months, my dad had made it clear that he did not want me to go to Union Seminary. He got his good friend and predecessor at Marble Church, Rev. Daniel Poling, to take me to lunch at the Union League Club in New York to talk to me about this matter. Why, asked Poling, did I, someone from a good conservative religious background, want to go to Union Seminary? Union had the reputation of being a liberal, social-action-oriented seminary and of high quality with influential faculty members, including Reinhold Niebuhr. I was attracted to it for its academic reputation and its progressive view of Christianity, which was conveyed in a periodical from the seminary named *Christianity and Crisis*. I was especially impressed by one project from Union—the East Harlem Protestant Parish, a storefront church doing Christian work on the streets of Harlem.

I do not recall specific conversations between me and my dad about this topic. I decided on my own to go to this seminary, partly because it was in New York City, but particularly because of its academic reputation and its distinguished faculty. I was unaware of the depth of my dad's negative opinion about the seminary. So I was surprised and shocked to receive the following curt letter from him on this subject: "Dear John, I cannot understand why you are going into the seat of my most implacable enemies. Love, Dad." This letter and my reaction to it led me into a web of confusion and anger.

To be sure this was an enormously difficult time for my dad. The idea for the group that Dad ended up leading in New York originally emanated from the Billy Graham organization and the National Association for Evangelicals. Billy was in Switzerland; Dad became the chair and spokesperson for this group in New York City. As I have indicated, it generated much publicity and was in the news, and in a sense, it was the talk of the town. Unbeknownst to me then, Dad took the heat for all the criticism that came, in no way saying that the impetus for the group came from others. He was personally stung and left reeling from the barrage of criticism, and he actively took the step of writing and submitting his resignation as minister of Marble Collegiate Church. The board of Marble Church refused even to consider it.

One of the reasons I was largely unaware of all that was happening to my dad was that this summer was of great importance to me personally. Earlier that year, on June 25, 1960, my parents journeyed to Lynchburg, Virginia, to attend Lydia's and my wedding in the Rivermont Presbyterian Church, where her father, Rev. Edgar A. Woods, was minister. My father assisted in the wedding, and so we faced both our fathers at the altar. Everyone seemed to be happy; certainly, we were. At the rehearsal dinner the night before, my dad took the hosting responsibilities and played it cool and fun by asking each person there what brought them to Lynchburg on this occasion. I recall that my uncle Leonard said, "The grace of God and the invitation of the family." Uncle Leonard was Dad's younger brother, and his humor was typical of that of the Peale men.

After the wedding, Lydia and I were off on our honeymoon at an inn next to the front entrance of the Homestead Hotel in Hot Springs,

Virginia. My parents returned to their lives in New York. We were having a memorable, loving, and happy time getting started in our marriage. Later that summer, Lydia and I took a trip to visit my cousin Bobby Peale, son of Dad's brother Bob, who was a minister in a Methodist Church in Scottsdale, Arizona. Our trip across the country was fun and interesting, but our trip back was hurried, as Lydia needed to report to a job that opened up for her at Dwight School for Girls in Englewood, New Jersey. The final day of the trip was a long drive from Kankakee, Illinois, to Pawling, New York, where we stayed with my parents.

Only then did we begin to realize how difficult a time it was for my dad, as it was when he was writing out his resignation from the Marble Church. He was deeply conflicted about what was happening with what was then called "the Peale Group" and the storm of criticism it aroused. Lydia and I were working and living at my parents' home on Quaker Hill. At this time, my parents were in Switzerland, where there was the important meeting of Christian "evangelicals." It was not until comparatively recently that I became aware of the specific events and actions of Dad and others that led to the trouble that hit the newspapers after the Washington meeting.

In the summer of 1960, the National Association of Evangelicals (NEA) became an active player forming a position on the campaign. Rev. Donald Gill, a Baptist minister, was given the task of organizing a group, which took the name of Citizens for Religious Freedom. On August 18 in Montreux,, Switzerland, there was a meeting of about twenty-five leading evangelicals from the NEA. These planners saw the need for a large public meeting, including Gill's group, which would take place in Washington. My dad chaired this group, and after the meeting, a prepared statement was issued with a five-point criticism of the politics of the Roman Catholic Church.

The position paper seriously questioned whether a Roman Catholic president would be able to withstand the concerted efforts of the Roman Catholic Church hierarchy, and it suggested that having a Roman Catholic president would certainly be a blow to religious liberty for Americans.

With all of this going on, Lydia and I walked into the Seminary on this early September afternoon, the day after the Washington meeting. Although I did not know then many of the specifics of his time of difficulty, what I did know was the most important thing: I loved him and was loyal to him and his work. I was in pain to see him hurt so much. I wanted to be close to him, yet it was my lot to have to live with the pain of separation and the loss of genuine contact with him. In comparison to his problems, it didn't seem to matter much that this was a difficult time for me also.

I did well at Union Theological Seminary, in full attendance from 1960 to graduation in 1963. I especially enjoyed the distinguished Union faculty, taking courses and getting to know such high-quality theological professionals as Robert McAfee Brown and Daniel Day Williams in theology, Cyril Richardson and Wilhelm Pauck in church history, James Muilenberg and Samuel Terrien in Old Testament, Louis Martyn in New Testament, and so many more. It was fun to try to figure out if Pauck was teaching Luther or Luther was teaching Pauck. Robert Horn taught courses in Plato and the Platonic tradition, which I enjoyed with relish. It was at Union that I absorbed even more of the theology of Paul Tillich.

It was there that I had the exciting and stimulating experience of really reading Soren Kierkegaard in a highly concentrated way, mostly in his works: *Philosophical Fragments, Concluding Unscientific Postscript to the Philosophical Fragments*, and, of course, *Fear and Trembling*. Kierkegaard's life and work has had a powerful and long-lasting influence on my thinking and my Christian life. His stages on life's way—especially his treatment of the story of Abraham in Genesis, chapter 22—have been so helpful to me in my understanding and my religious development. I was also enormously influenced by Cyril Richardson, who helped give me a solid foundation in Church history and the history of Christian theology, especially the several important Christian thinkers up to and beyond Augustine, a pivotal figure who has been highly influential on me and my work.

Lydia and I had fun and memorable times with our many friends— for example, Tom and Brenda Stiers. One night we received a note under our door, saying that the word was out that Lydia's "rabbit test" was positive. Brenda was also pregnant. The note was unsigned, but I soon traced it down to Tom and confronted him. To properly consider this matter, we went down Broadway to a popular local bar to share our news together. It was a place he and I frequented, often saying we had to go looking for somewhere to buy stamps to mail our letters.

It was not long before we met and became acquainted with Professor Bennett. One night early in our time at Union, I was out doing my Field Work at Riverside Church, just across the street from Union, and

Lydia was cleaning our small apartment at Hastings Hall at Union. This residence hall had been designed for single men pre-WWI, and it was, to be sure, quite small for a couple. Lydia, with mop in hand and with our stuff out in the hallway, greeted John Bennett, who had come to meet us. He was friendly and soon thereafter invited us both to dinner with him and his wife in their faculty apartment. It is interesting that Bennett at Union and Dad at Marble Collegiate Church are relatively near together in New York, but yet so far apart.

Our relations with my parents during these years still seemed good. Once when Mother was away, we entertained Dad in our modest new home, a pleasant occasion. We also visited them for dinner once when the male star of the movie *One Man's Way*, named Don Murray, also attended. That movie was about Dad's life. Before dinner, we took our new baby girl, Laura, to their apartment, and they babysat while we went to the Guggenheim Museum for a time away for us. I do remember one sour note, however. At that dinner, as I made a comment about theology during our discussion, I felt put down by Dad, who seemed to have no interest in any such type of inquiry.

In my Union years, I continued to be proud and loving toward my dad, in spite of the critical views about him by John Bennett and many others. I defended him on occasion, but mostly I entered into the theological swirl with enthusiasm and a strong desire to learn. Toward the end of my time at Union, there was a sense about me that I had come from a background different from that of Union thinking and had maintained my integrity.

With respect to Dad, I formed the view, which I have had for years, that I could be close to him even though there were disagreements, and in spite of the independence on my part. That thought became a big problem for me, for it became increasingly clear that Dad did not share it, or at least he didn't show that he shared it. In this light, I learned an important lesson from that chief critic, John Bennett. He sharply criticized people's point of view, as he did with Dad, but he held a sincere Christian love in his heart for those same people, including Norman Vincent Peale. I don't believe that Dad was capable of such a virtue. Perhaps Dad felt that a difference of opinion with him amounted to a rejection of him. This was part of his insecurity. He felt inferior to academicians and felt that he couldn't and didn't want to debate with them. Perhaps his small-town, midwestern values kicked in at this point. He seemed uncomfortable in sophisticated settings. It is so apparent to me now how even in these painful and ambivalent circumstances, and perhaps because of them, I was experiencing significant personal development in my own becoming.

In the summer of 1959, I had gone with our family to Europe and the Holy Land. Again in 1961, the Peale family led a large pilgrimage to the Holy Land, with my parents present on both trips. Lydia came along on the second trip. As I remember it, I seemed to be close to Dad on those occasions. I prepared an extensive set of notes for all the people on the tour of biblical sites and history, as well as a Bible study plan and spiritual reflections and prayers. Dad, along with the others, including my sister Eliz, appreciated this. We were in sync on many occasions, as for example, when we sat on the mountain overlooking the Sea of Galilee, where tradition has it that Jesus preached the "Sermon on the Mount." With everyone seated in a small area, I read Matthew, chapters 5–7, from the New Testament. I could see that Dad was moved, as was I. He was present during the many devotions I gave in the American Colony Hotel, and I felt his approval for me and my sisters.

On one occasion we met with King Hussein, and since Dad had other obligations, he was forced to miss the occasion. I was proud to represent him at that meeting, standing before the king, where etiquette required that my head be lower than his. I said "Your Majesty," and speaking well for the group. The second of these two pilgrimage trips was in the summer after my first year at Union Seminary in New York. It too was a memorable and precious time, as I had many experiences, such as my walk from the village of Bethany over the Mount of Olives.

Chapter 9: Becoming in My Studies and My Life as a Professor

Chicago and Elmhurst College in Illinois

After I graduated from Union Seminary, I felt like I was sitting on the top of a fence, wondering which way I was going to fall off. On the one side was the Christian ministry, the inspirational goal of being a minister like my dad. On the other side was the academic life, the inspiring goal of becoming a professor of philosophy. Feeling a strong pull in both directions put me in a state of internal tension. If I chose the former, then perhaps I could serve as a minister of the gospel and find and regain what I had lost in my relationship with Dad. If I chose the academic side, I would be doing what I had come to think was what I really wanted. This is another way of stating and even reliving the basic tension in my life.

During this time in my life I was unclear and ambivalent about my relation to my dad. I felt like I was growing apart from him while trying to find my own way in academics, and at the same time, I loved him. So there was a battle going on in me, a sort of push-pull that propelled me to seek the closeness I had experienced as a boy. At the same time, I felt repelled, as I realized how self-absorbed and self-important he had become. I had this inner conflict, yet I was the son of Norman Vincent Peale. It seemed to me that I had to keep this private in the recesses of my own tortured soul, for who would understand how the son of the man who wrote the book on positive thinking could be so conflicted and negative! I lived in fear that for me to be open with this kind of torment would cause people to think that there was something wrong with positive thinking. Perhaps there is.

At Union, I took a program of courses designed for future teachers, but I was still on the fence emotionally. I went to Chicago to find out which one would be my option. First, I enrolled at the University of Chicago, taking many fine courses, which I still value and remember with a sense of importance. I took a course on Aristotle from Richard McKeon, a noted Aristotle scholar. Those who want to know what that felt like should read the novel *Zen and the Art of Motorcycle Maintenance*, written by Robert Pirsig, who also took this course. Professor McKeon would propose a passage from Aristotle, asking the students to give a proper exposition. Going around the room, he found deficiencies in the reports of each student, including me. Then Professor McKeon would profess the truth! We were all suitably humbled, but we learned in spite of him.

I also took a course with Professor Alan Gewirth on selected issues in ethics, such as justice and the good, as reflected in important writings in the history of philosophy. Another exciting course was that offered by Dudley Shapere, who wrote a review and lectured on one of the most highly influential books of the second half of the twentieth century—*The Structure of Scientific Revolutions*, by Thomas Kuhn. Shapere's course was one of the finest courses I ever took, even considering those of Professor Myers at Washington and Lee. For years, my own course, Philosophy of Science, was modeled after that offered by Professor Shapere.

The most important personal thing that happened to Lydia and me in Chicago was the birth of our second and third children, both in Michael Reese Hospital. The most important professional thing for me, however, was the securing of my first teaching job at Elmhurst College in Elmhurst, Illinois, to the west of Chicago. I wanted to find out if I really wanted to teach, so I taught there. I found out that I really loved it, and more interestingly, that I was good at it. I developed a fine course in Introduction to Philosophy, and also the Philosophy of Science, among others.

It was good for me to find out that although I felt inspired and challenged when preaching in a church context, I felt like I was more naturally myself when teaching. I came to use a method of challenging students with questions and seeking to help them discover their own answers as I was discovering mine. Although I didn't know this at the time, I was being driven further away from my dad by favoring teaching over preaching. At this time, I felt as I always felt—that he, as a parent, might take an interest in what I, his son, was finding as my own way. That sensitivity on his part surfaced only once in my whole career, and that, in the long run, was a bitter disappointment for me.

I found that I could teach in such a way that good, stimulating discussions were drawn out of the students. I modeled my teaching on the Socratic method of being a "midwife" of the ideas of my students, to draw from them their own questions and discussion of options for answers. For the most part, the students responded well to my work. I really cared about them, about their learning and their development in thinking and maturing as persons.

For me, teaching became a form of ministry, a ministry in academia, and my personal associations with so many students gave me the opportunity to help them develop their own thinking and their faith. I was not then, nor was I ever, one of those liberal-minded professors who tore down the faith of impressionable young people. I hadn't yet grown a beard, nor had I put leather patches on my elbows, nor did I smoke a pipe. Much of that would come later to fill out the trappings of professorship!

My dad and mother once visited one of my classes at Elmhurst College, sitting in the back of the room, as inconspicuous as they could be, smiling approvingly as I taught the subject of aesthetics. Dad was enthusiastic and happy about what I did that day. It was a memorable experience, which happened, I believe, in the fall of 1967 on the ground floor of Hammerschmidt Chapel at Elmhurst College. The classroom was a large room with student chairs in rows behind the teacher's desk and a podium behind which was a long chalkboard. There were about twenty-five students present, and they did not seem to have any particular awareness that a celebrity was present. I tried and succeeded to pay little or no attention to my parents, even though they stood out, dressed as they were in formal business attire. As I remember it, I was quite focused on my work, highly engaged in the subject matter, which was interesting to me. I was lecturing and raising questions, and I was pleased that student questions and discussions came readily. It was an especially good class, and I was happy for that.

I don't recall being angry at Dad on that day, but instead happy that he could witness my work firsthand. It gave me hope that he might begin to take some interest in and support my decision to make teaching my career. It turned out to be false hope. The joy turned sour later as I came to be aware that this moment was the one and only time he encouraged me in my entire thirty-year career in teaching! What a downer this realization was for me. It took me down into the depths of despair later in my life.

I also remember that Dad led a bit of a celebratory event at the publication of my first book, *Biblical History as the Quest for Maturity*. The trouble was that the only other comment I ever heard from him on my book was a remark he made to an associate: "Did you ever try to read John's book?" Of course, sadly to say, Dad never talked to me about my book or showed me that he really cared about what I said or what I meant. As far as I know, he made no effort to understand or appreciate the outlook I was endeavoring to develop.

I like to compare that comment of Dad's, which hurt me greatly, to a remark later in my career, when I overheard a student at another college talking about how I was one of the two philosopher kings on campus. To me, that meant that I had achieved my goal of becoming like Dr. Myers.

The University of North Carolina at Chapel Hill

I went to the University of North Carolina at Chapel Hill in 1968 to earn my PhD, which I did in the early 1970s. This university was a good match for me, as I had fine professors in a congenial atmosphere for academic work. The town of Chapel Hill was also an amenable place for our young family to live. Our children began to grow up there. They started school there. We had a good family experience in our modest home on Hickory Drive. We rented that house by a shake-of-the-hand agreement with the owner, for only $130 per month. Our whole family still has many Chapel Hill friends. Of no small importance to us is that we all became strong supporters and fans of the UNC men's basketball Tar Heel team, then under Coach Dean Smith. As a family, we still have this passion.

I was successful in my goal of becoming "Dr. Peale" at UNC. Immediately after I passed my oral exam for my dissertation on "The Theory of Belief," a faculty member called me "Dr. Peale." Instinctively, I turned around to see if Dad was behind me! Unfortunately, Dad had not been behind me for any of my own journey toward my goal. I don't recall anything like congratulations on my earning this highest of academic degrees. Needless to say, I *earned* a PhD, noting in my thinking that Dad only received "honorary" degrees.

I have very few recollections of approval or encouragement from Dad and Mother, except that of financial support. Needless to say, this was very important to us, enabling us to do many things that wouldn't have been possible—like sending each of our children to fine, small liberal arts colleges, Kenyon, Williams, and Dickinson. Later in life, the continued support enabled us to live comfortably so that we were not in financial need. On the other hand, it was almost never clear to me that I could count on emotional or spiritual support from them. To me, this kind of sustenance was most important, and from my parents it was sorely lacking.

While I loved my dad, ironically this increased my inner turmoil. I never really considered walking away from them emotionally or spiritually, and I continued to hope, increasingly as the years went on, that Dad would realize that I was doing good things in life and appreciate me for that. I was inspiring classes of students rather than congregations of church goers, and what is wrong with a career like that? Of course, the purse strings, especially at a time when I was just starting out at Elmhurst College on a small salary, and now was in graduate school seeking to earn a PhD, were important considerations, tying me more closely to them on a regular basis. Resentment over the purse strings as a major connection with my parents began to cause inner turmoil of a different sort.

In all my educational institutions along the way, I had fine professors and fine courses. I looked to them as models for my own career, not to mention my own life. I appreciate these sensitive people, teachers and scholars, for their influence on me as a student and as a maturing person. The influence of these people, whom I will never forget, has been a major factor in my becoming.

I remember most vividly David Falk, a German who had first gone to Oxford to get the academic status of a "First," which he did. Then he came to the University of North Carolina at Chapel Hill. His subtle humor and devotion to his philosophical work impressed and challenged me in a creative way. Things he said to me showed that he cared for me and looked toward a successful career for me. His courses in the philosophy of David Hume provided some of the most important influences of my entire career. Hume's philosophy gave me insight into so many of the problems of philosophy. One of these problems was that of skepticism regarding knowledge.

In the tradition of British empiricism, Hume followed Locke and Berkeley. In Hume's philosophy, skepticism reached its high point, especially in knowledge of the self. Hume said, in effect, whenever he "entered into what he called his self," he never "stumbled on some particular impression or another, but did not find himself distinct from some such impression." Ideas are based on impressions, so, empirically, there is no certain knowledge of the self. For years, this sort of thinking challenged me and drove me to think and work out positions of my own in my own field of philosophy. I am proud to be connected indirectly with Immanuel Kant, who says he was awakened by Hume's skeptical challenge "from his dogmatic slumbers." In my development as a teacher, it was stimulating for me and my students to take a stance with Hume to probe deeply into so many problems in philosophy.

Also there was Richard Smyth, with his fine courses in Modern Philosophy, and also Douglas Long, whose perspicacity and insight were so stimulating for me. Dr. Long served as the first reader of my dissertation on "The Theory of Belief." There was also Maynard Adams, a Kenan Professor of Philosophy at UNC, who was a second reader of my dissertation and the mentor for whom I was a teaching assistant. I became quite familiar with his philosophical system in his courses. When talking with Maynard, I realized that he was plugging me into some point in his philosophical system, and I learned to move with him, gaining understanding and illumination.

When he had to be absent for his classes, I would fill in, a duty I loved and honored. He once told me that I had been the best teaching assistant that he had ever had. Years later when he was using a cane, and I had developed my thinking more maturely, he came to a church in Chapel Hill to hear me preach. He said that I showed keen insight, and he gave me a hug, just about the last thing I would have expected from this formal and distinguished professor!

During my early life after college, as I have written, I had been on the fence between careers in the ministry in church and teaching in the classroom in academia. Clearly I was favoring the latter and made my decision for that pursuit in life, but even in my later years, I still have the desire to preach and be active in church affairs. In this sense, the influence of my dad and the inspiration from him has been a constant in my life, even though it also filled me with woe. The disturbing tension I felt during my early career has turned into a creative tension, a stimulating point of departure in my work.

During one of my classes as a teaching assistant at the University of North Carolina, there was on a certain day a distinct lack of good attendance. I found out that Jane Fonda was on campus that day. She had a greater draw for the students than did my philosophy class! At another time, during this Vietnam War period, a representative of the DOW Chemical Company came to speak to the hostile university crowd, which included me. He tried to soften our attitudes with humor, saying that he was "one of those callous Dowboys."

These were difficult days in our country's history. The killing of a girl and others on the grassy knoll at Kent State occurred in 1971, an event that became known as the "May 4th Massacre." This was a difficult time at the University of North Carolina and at many other universities. Our university, like many others, effectively closed down during this time, the spring semester of 1971.

On a more academic note, I was once in the university library, way down in the bowels of the stacks, taking out a book titled *The Ethics of Belief* by W. K. Clifford, an intellectual opponent of William James. No one else had checked out the book for a long time. I blew the dust off it and checked it out because of its relation to William James, the very same writer Dad was advised to read by Professor Arneson at Ohio Wesleyan University between 1916 and 1920. Dad had been advised to turn his life over to Jesus Christ and to check out books by William James in his library. I was doing the same in the bowels of the UNC library—except that I was checking out the work of a critic of James. While I was following Dad, I was also being more intellectually critical in becoming me.

During my time at Chapel Hill, I became a minister at the Church of Reconciliation. This experimental church was such an important place for our whole family, with so many good friends and such interesting and influential church experiences. The church was experimental in that it met in the cafeteria of a junior high school, with guitar as the main form of music and a liturgy that was flexible and discussion-friendly. For example, we used to have a break right after the sermon for open discussion of the sermon or of important issues in the life of the congregation. I did not think of this as any kind of rebellion away from the church manner of my parents, though they wouldn't have shared in the enthusiasm we had for such an open church. We also had a "church house" on the interface of the black and white communities in Chapel Hill and witnessed racial harmony in our interracial community.

The outpouring of love and care from the people in the Church of Reconciliation was nearly overwhelming. I was so touched when one of the members named Pat Hobson came to our home just as we were packing up to leave Chapel Hill for the continuing of my teaching career. He said that I had done something quite important at Chapel Hill and would be missed and remembered. Chapel Hill had been so important to us, and we miss and remember Pat and so many other friends. How good that experience was for us. Our daughter Lacy used to have a bumper sticker on her car that read: "If I owned heaven and Chapel Hill, I'd rent out heaven and live in Chapel Hill."

Chapter 10: Becoming in My Teaching Career

O ne of the things I am most proud of in my life is my teaching career of thirty years—indeed quite a successful career. One of the things that hurt me most and made me angriest was the almost complete lack of encouragement and support from my parents, except the financial support. I asked myself how it came to be that teaching was so natural and good for me. Why was I so naturally good at it? It certainly was not directly from my parents that the wherewithal to teach and to teach well came to me. I never took a course in how to teach, but I became a very good, prize-winning teacher, respected by students and faculty alike in every educational institution in which I worked.

As I have indicated, I had my first regular teaching appointment at Elmhurst College in 1965. While there, I had, on just one day, the only parental encouragement I ever received in my entire teaching career. They never called me up, as we call our children, asking how my work was going, seeking in some way to be involved or to guide me through personal difficulties on the job. The lack of parental involvement in my work hurt me and was a source of much anger and resentment. I never spoke to my parents or let them know this. Nor could I understand it.

What was wrong with becoming a professor? If my dad had problems of inferiority feelings relative to professors, surely that didn't mean that he couldn't support me in my own desire to be such a person. Apparently, I was wrong about that. My chosen profession was, it seemed, a major factor that caused him to pull away from me, for us to lose the close personal contact that we had in my early years. For years, the anger and resentment was something I could hold at bay, busy as I was in my development as an academician and college faculty type of person to the core. It was perhaps ironic that only in my later, more mature teaching years, and in my retirement, that I got so deeply angry about my father's attitude toward the life I had chosen and in which I was succeeding.

On the other hand, there are some things I got from him, some ways he influenced me and decidedly helped me to succeed in the very field he apparently couldn't tolerate. From him, I inherited, I believe, the capacity to speak well, in a public speaking sort of way, though for me it was in front of classes rather than in front of congregations. Also, like his father, Charles Clifford Peale, he had a naturalness about him that helped him to connect easily with people in an unaffected way. And he had a pastoral sense finely tuned over his entire career, wanting and being inclined to be a help to other people in a caring and loving way. I believe I inherited these capacities and talents from him.

In the final analysis, I suppose my dad just couldn't see beyond his own way of thinking and his own feelings to appreciate me in my chosen field in academia. It is said of him that he appreciated learning as a young student in college, but something happened to him. He read a great deal in his early years and studied influential and important thinkers and literary figures, especially poetry. But he and I never shared and mutually appreciated such things together. I just could not understand or accept that. Something happened in me, and it took me years to accept some very deep limitations and shortcomings of his. For years and through considerable emotional pain, I fought with and was frustrated by such thoughts as these.

It may be asked why I just couldn't accept him for what he was and was not, why my nascent realization of his limitations as a parent couldn't be stated and left at that. As I tried to show in my section on finding my own way, there was an anger that developed within me, which later led me into the depths of despair and darkness. This anger kept seething in the background of my mind and heart. I believe now that it was this factor that kept me from just accepting him as he was. The really difficult thing for me was that I felt this anger and despair and yet, all the while loving and respecting him. Somehow, seemingly miraculously, in my current state I still love him, yet the anger and darkness have largely gone out from me.

I have felt that I had a successful career. Yet I also felt that there was still something in me holding me back from fully developing my talents and capacities in my academic life and work. I believe now that this retardation in me came from my struggles with being on the fence between becoming a minister or a professor, between being in the church as a pastor or in the classroom as a teacher. I felt I had to struggle against a force within me that was holding me back from being the best I could be. Lack of parental encouragement and emotional support or practical involvement from early years negatively affects a child's self-esteem and deters his natural development. On a certain level, I was worrying about such things as these most, all during my early career.

Perhaps it was natural in some way that as I developed my own style and realized a good measure of success, I would be freer to let the anger come out more fully. There was something that I had to fight in the image and force of him in all my adult life. My ambivalence toward him, loving him, and being drawn to him ever since I was a boy, looking up at him and being inspired and proud—that was one side of me, a side that I have never lost, even now. Yet I also had a sense of struggle as I realized the disconnect from him. I regretted it and couldn't shake it, and later on, I became dominated by it. These inner tensions made it so that I couldn't focus clearly and totally on my own life's work. Living with this high level of frustration has been a big factor in my becoming.

After years, it just got to me and weighed me down so much that on a conscious level I quit fighting it. I just got more deeply angry and at the same time depressed at the high levels of negativity of his influence on me as I tried to be a good teacher and scholar. This is not to say that I didn't enjoy my teaching. On a certain level, I loved it and was proud of my accomplishments as a teacher. I have a professional lifetime of memories of classroom experiences and relations with students out of class to savor and enjoy in my retirement. I even had moments when students were to me as I had been to the many professors I have praised, especially to Dr. Myers at Washington and Lee University. I have sensed the respect and the desire to learn from these students, just as I respected Myers. I have given of myself for their betterment through the learning process all through my career. This has given me a solid pride and satisfaction in my accomplishments throughout my teaching career.

In my teaching, there were three things I wanted my students to know about me: first, that I was knowledgeable in my subject matter of philosophy and that I loved it; second, that in my courses, it was difficult to get an A or high B grade; and third, that I really cared about the students themselves, believing that by learning this material, they would be developing important qualities for themselves in their lives.

I believed that my enthusiasm about my subject matter would carry over and be communicated to my students. I thought that they too might be inspired to have a professor who so obviously was so much into his own subject matter. I also believe that a caring and loving attitude from me would likewise be contagious. Learning for them in my classes was never only a matter of understanding the readings or the course content. I wanted them to see how the teaching in my classes could be interesting and liberating in their own lives. Such is the meaning in teaching the "liberal arts," such as philosophy.

Over the years, I developed fine courses in philosophy, of which I am proud. First and foremost was my Introduction to Philosophy course. This was constructed in such a way that in response to various philosophical problems, I would weave several lines of answers, which put together would be alternative philosophies the students could hold to deal with all these problems in a single philosophical perspective. They could then emerge from this first course with the makings of a philosophical point of view.

My starting point was the problems most likely, I thought, to engage or grab the students' interest. I started with ourselves, our human nature, our bodies and spirits or souls, and how or what we are as persons. From this, I went on to questions a self-conscious person might ask: "Where did I come from? What am I now? And how can I become and do the best that is in me?" So we talked about problems in the philosophy of religion, philosophical psychology or the philosophy of mind, and morality and ethics.

I developed other good courses in all the standard divisions of the field. Professor Shapere's course that I thought so well of at the University of Chicago was the basis of my own Philosophy of Science course. My work in the Philosophy of Mind at North Carolina led me to develop interesting and engaging courses in this field. There was my Aesthetics course, which was always fun and interesting. It was also important for me that my students learn the history of philosophy in courses like Ancient Philosophy, Medieval and Renaissance Philosophy, and philosophy in both the modern and contemporary periods.

Two of my three children, Laura and Lacy, each called me up as they were studying for their own courses, Ethics and the History of Philosophy, in college. We had good talks over the telephone. They told me that I was saying what their professors were saying, and my explanations helped them. One time, Laura called from Kenyon College, saying that she was stuck at an important place in her course, Ancient Philosophy. Without any hesitation, I responded that she was stuck in the puzzles set up by what may be called "the post-Heraclitean-Parmenidean Problem." It was this problem that Plato and Aristotle and other important ancient philosophers set out to answer in the development of their own philosophies. I gave Laura insights into the problem and thus into the most influential answers to this problem in the history of philosophy. For Laura, as for my own students, fully understanding this problem is a great accomplishment.

Whenever I would meet my students, I would seek to keep alive a restless and searching spirit of inquiry, something I wanted very much for myself. Students in my courses would hang around after classes. Or we would talk in my office or around on the campus. This kind of curiosity was one of the things in my paternal grandfather, Charles Clifford Peale, that I so admired. Unhappily, I never shared with my father any such thing. As I see it, he was too busy being famous and important, and he was not there for me. Obviously, however, I was not there for him either, as in his view, I had gone my own way, away from what he was endeavoring to do in his life and work. What a pity—what a shame for both of us. I suppose we both hurt from this psychological distance from each other. God knows that I was hurt. I don't really know how, if at all, he was bothered by this. He never opened up to me with any such thoughts. What I do know is how I became angered and depressed. The realization of all this came slowly, creeping, as I now see it, from my unconscious or preconscious into to my awareness.

There is much more about my teaching and my courses that can be told. Due to a difficult job market in the early and mid-1970s, I started working some temporary jobs. While working on my degree at the University of North Carolina, I taught for some time at Stratford College in Danville, Virginia, where I felt the love of my work come to the fore as I engaged good students in philosophical pursuits. There were a series of one-year jobs until in 1976 I landed a long-term position at Longwood

College, in Farmville, Virginia, now Longwood University. I taught at Longwood for twenty-three good and professionally productive years.

One morning in Farmville, I woke up to the fact that I had arrived at a place I had always wanted to be, that is a "full" professor of philosophy. I had become a Dr. Myers on campus for many students. It was there that I overheard one of my students, named Victor, say, "Peale is one of the two best teachers and scholars on campus." At Longwood, I received two awards, the first of which came about at my fourth year, a teacher of the year type of reward "in recognition of professional excellence and devoted service to students." Later on, in the year of my retirement, I received the highest award given by the university, the citation in the same vein as the earlier award, with the addition of "distinguished service to the institution."

It was during my time at Longwood University that I took my second sabbatical to go to China and teach with Lydia at the Foreign Affairs College in Beijing. Later, due to serious health issues, we decided that I had to retire, which I did in 1999. Lydia retired from the teaching of English at Prince Edward County High School, and I from Longwood University. Earlier in 1994, we had decided that we needed to make a residential move, which took us to the Charlottesville, Virginia, area, specifically Lake Monticello, in neighboring Fluvanna County. I commuted to work at Longwood on a reduced teaching schedule for five years before my early retirement at age sixty-two. At that time, I was experiencing the onset of serious health issues. These health problems came with the announcement to me by two different doctors of three different types of cancer that had developed in me during the 1990s.

Of course, Lydia and I remember neither recognition nor involvement of my parents at the time of my retirement and the conclusion of my successful teaching career. I retired after the 1998–1999 academic year at Longwood, my twenty-third year of teaching there. This occurred six years after my dad passed away on December 24, 1993. Mother was too old to be aware of such things. This was no problem. But what *was* a problem for me was that there was almost no recognition or involvement or encouragement from Dad the whole way through.

Perhaps he was self-absorbed and had lost the ability to step outside himself and his fame and success to have a human connection with me. Maybe he was just too busy or hid behind his busyness. I can accept this conclusion now as I write these words. At the time and for years ahead up into the turn of the century, I was plagued with hurt, anger, and depression. At the onset of my bottom came darkness and the desperation that comes with active alcoholism.

During my time at Longwood, Lydia was teaching English at the Prince Edward County High School. She became a distinguished teacher of English, sharing with a teacher of history in a joint course for the most advanced students. Our three children came to Farmville. Clifford and Lacy entered the Longwood Campus School in the seventh and fifth grades, respectively. Laura entered Prince Edward High School in the tenth grade. She graduated from high school in 1980. Clifford and Lacy came to Prince Edward and graduated in 1983 and 1985. All three children had their mother as an English teacher. This produced some interesting episodes. Our children, as students, would say to their teacher-mother, "What do you mean by giving us a B+ grade?" Upon occasion, Lydia would act unwisely by asking the kids how she did in class that day. Fun times ensued in the family discussions about these issues!

Chapter 11: Becoming in My Travels

Traveling abroad has been a facet of my life and that of my sisters from the very beginning, that was encouraged and supported by our parents. In the family history, it was clear that my parents also journeyed abroad and throughout the United States and had valued their trips. Exciting and interesting family talk was often held about the grandeur of other countries and the interesting history and cultures of ancient civilizations. As we three children grew up in the family, such trips continued, and some were grand and exciting trips, many of them planned and organized by Mother. Early on, I remember my dad talking with pride about how his mother, Anna Delaney, had journeyed to the Far East, including the Philippines and China. My parents gave us important and generous financial support for our own many travels.

My first trip on my own was in the summer of 1954, when I went with two Deerfield friends, Peter Sellar and George Allen, to a salmon fishery in the north of Scotland near Inverness on the bay of the Findhorn River. Our life there was focused on catching salmon as they headed up the river to spawn. We rowed out into the mouth of the river, with the nets trailing out back of the boat in a large circle out from and back to land. There we attached the net ropes to a winch and pulled in the salmon, and the net came to shore. It was hard work, and it was fun; we were thankful when there were royal decrees that limited such work on some weekends. We three boys got to know that section of Scotland very well.

We enjoyed our associations with the Brown Scottish family who were our hosts. When they wanted to talk about things out of our ken, they used Scottish brogue in a way that we could not understand them. We learned Scottish songs, ate Scottish trifles and other delectables, and thoroughly enjoyed ourselves. Afterward, we had the chance to go to London and Paris before returning to reality back home. Peter Sellar is still my friend, living close by in Virginia.

The summer of 1954 was my interlude between high school at Deerfield Academy and college at Washington and Lee University. It was such a good time of my life. Since then, I have traveled to approximately fifty-seven countries in Europe, the Middle East, Africa, South America, Central America, Canada, and the Far East—including, most importantly for us, to China. My last trip to China was in 2008, fifty-four years after my first excursion to Scotland!

All those trips and the rich and varied experiences in them shaped me in my becoming as I was growing up. It is personally broadening to experience and absorb foreign cultures and customs. One gets a wider sense of the varieties of human life and of diverse cultural patterns, which is deeply educational. It contributes significantly to a maturing and expanding awareness of history when one has the opportunity to feel the ancient cultures come alive, being at a place where so many important events occurred. It helps one to learn of one's own culture and to see it in comparison and contrast with others, some of which are so vastly different.

The family trip to the Holy Land in 1959 and the "pilgrimage" we made to the Holy Land in 1961 and again in 1987 were quite significant. These were trips on which my parents came along, and it was good to be with them at such inspiring places. I have vivid and powerful memories of these visits. On the second of these holy journeys, perhaps in 1961, I took a taxi one day from the city of Jerusalem to the village of Bethany, on the side of the Mount of Olives. I walked back, finding what looked like a very old roadway up the back side of the Mount, to the top and then down toward Jerusalem. I imagined it an old Roman road. From the top of the Mount of Olives, I could get a wonderful, awe-inspiring view of the Holy City of Jerusalem, lit up as it was on this occasion by the light of the setting sun.

I walked down the mountain, passing with prayer and meditation the place where tradition has it that Jesus wept over the city. Reaching the bottom of the mountain, I came into the Garden of Gethsemane and paused for a time of my own prayer and meditation. I prayed that in my life I could say as Jesus did at this place, "Not my will but thine be done."

I crossed the Kidron Valley, entering into one of the gates of the Holy City, set on a hill, and made my way along the twelve Stations of the Cross to the house of Caiaphas, ruler of the Sanhedrin, the High Council of the Jews, where Peter was when Jesus was inside being questioned and challenged by the council. This was where they were seeking a way to assign the death penalty and where Peter was in the process of denying his Lord three times before the cock crowed. I was lost in my own spiritual sorrow at the condition of those of us who follow Jesus but leave him alone to die.

Then with the family, I took a prayerful and contemplative trip through the twelve Stations of the Cross. As I recall, there was only once when we hesitated. Mother seemed to break for us the religiously somber mood of our trek, as she stopped and took some interest in browsing in the Simon of Cyrene dress shop!

We journeyed all the way to the Church of the Holy Sepulcher, the traditional site of Golgotha, the place of crucifixion. What a deep, religious experience this was!

During the course of these two trips, we traveled widely through Israel, Jordan, Lebanon, and even Syria, not to mention the mountains on the east side of the Jordan River Valley. We traveled from Dan to Beersheba, from the snows of Mt. Hermon in the north to the desert fortress of Massada in the south. From west to east, we journeyed from the coast of the Mediterranean to Mt. Nebo and across from the cedars of Lebanon to the Becca Valley and even on the Road to Damascus, where Paul had his experience of the risen Lord, and where we came to a sign in English, saying "Welcome to Syria!"

We went again to Jerusalem in the late 1980s. On this trip, we sang Christmas carols in the shepherds' fields outside Bethlehem in a Christmas service of the YMCA. In all of these Holy Land experiences, I had a rich sense of the presence of my dad, who inspired in me such awe for the land that is holy and in taking my walk with Jesus.

On these trips, there were predominately good relations between me and my parents and our greater family. To appreciate the sights, smells, and tastes of the Holy Land, and to share that with my mother and dad, was an enlivening and deepening experience for us all. We could delight and learn together, comparably free from the existing emotional ambivalence and tension in my soul, and maybe in spite of it.

Our parents took us on another Christmas trip, this one to Kenya, in the late 1980s. There we sang our Christmas carols around a fire by a river filled with hippopotami. It was a bit of a stretch. One early morning on this trip, Lydia and I awoke and pulled back our tent flaps to see the morning sunlight on the "Snows of Kilimanjaro," with thoughts of Hemingway in our minds. It was fun and different for me and my sisters to see our father adjusting to a safari tent, even a fancy one, in the jungle, where at night our campsite was encircled with a ring of fire to keep dangerous animals at bay.

Lydia and I took two other trips to Africa. At one point, we stood on the southern tip of the continent, viewing the convergence of the Indian and Atlantic Oceans. On this trip to the Cape of Good Hope, we passed a sign that read something like "5,783 miles to Washington, DC"! On yet another trip to Africa, in Egypt, we journeyed from Alexandria in the north to Abu Simel in the south and from the Nile to one of the four places where Helena, the mother of Constantine, built churches over what were then the four major sites in the Holy Land—the monastery of St. Catherine at the foot of Gaba Musa, the mountain where, according to tradition, Moses viewed the bush that was burning but was not consumed. How rich in history, how inspiring was all of this to us! How deepening a religious sense that we were led into in this land.

Our many other exciting trips included a journey from Rio De Janeiro in Brazil below the high mountain with the statue of Christ, all the way south to the Falkland Islands. We were on a small cruise boat where the crew members were all naturalists. What a pleasant and interesting learning environment this was. We made "wet landings" off our catamarans onto islands to study flora, fauna, and living things. We visited Buenos Aires in Argentina, and we went on a tour of a ranch to watch the horsemen ride in their own spectacular way and to feed our faces with juicy Argentine steaks.

At the end of that trip, we flew across the Andes to Santiago, Chile, and went to Asuncion, the capital city of Paraguay, to visit a cousin of Lydia's and to go to the great waterfall at Iguazu, the "Great Water" along the border lands of Paraguay, Argentina, and Brazil. This reminded us of that fine movie, *The Mission*, about the Catholic Jesuit who went to missionize the natives above the falls, and the ultimate failure of that mission. We were reminded of another great waterfall in Africa, at Victoria Falls, "The smoke that thunders." Appreciation of such sights as these has become part of my personal development, enlivening my imagination and widening my horizons and deepening my understanding.

One of the exciting things about even the idea of taking such trips is the example set for us by our parents, who relished the same sorts of excitements. Directly or indirectly, we felt closer to them in the spirit of adventure and learning that such trips fostered.

There were other trips over most all of Europe, and to Central America, to the Orient, to the Philippines, and Bangkok in Thailand, and to Siem Reap in Cambodia, not to mention Katmandu in Nepal. One crystal clear fall day in Katmandu, I took an hour-long flight toward and quite near the major Himalayan Mountains, including Everest looming high in the background. What spectacular sights were these! For some reason, Lydia chose not to go on this trip with me. I imagined people climbing these mountains, ascending to the heights in their own lives just because the mountains were there. I was stimulated in my effort to climb the heights in my own life.

Several of the European trips were organized and paid for by my parents. We enjoyed important family times, particularly in Switzerland at Interlaken and Zermatt. It was in Interlaken, Switzerland, on a family trip that we all celebrated the fiftieth wedding anniversary of our parents. We all gathered around the dinner table in a private dining room, telling stories and having a loving and celebrative time.

Chapter 12: Becoming in My Discovery of China

*S*uddenly, *I found something new and passionate in my life* that had little to do with my dad or my mother, and the new engagement was such a relief from the constant nagging ambivalence and struggle over my relation to my dad. On a conscious level, I was not aware of this being my own thing, but that is the way it turned out. I have come to realize that I was looking for something for myself that was stimulating and different from the rest of my life. To find something not motivated as a reaction against my dad, or even in comparison with him, was important for me. What happened to me was that I discovered China and became deeply fascinated by China and the Chinese. My life has not quite been the same ever since that first discovery.

In 1985, on our twenty-fifth wedding anniversary, Lydia and I took a grand tour to China on a trip sponsored by Yale and Cornell Universities. We took what has become the usual sort of excursion to what have become regular tourist spots in China. We were fortunate to have two professors, an American historian of China from Cornell and a most unusual Chinese person who was a sociologist from Yale. Their lectures and discussions were quite insightful.

As far as my motivations were concerned, it is noteworthy that we were following my wife's parents, who had been missionaries in China in the 1930s. Lydia was born in China in 1936 in Jiangsu Province, in a city now called Suqian. The family had a long and distinguished career in Christian and medical missions in China over many years, perhaps as many as three hundred plus, for the service-work of all the members of the wider family. We were following the work of Lydia's father, Rev. Edgar A. Woods, and certain of her uncles and aunts in various places we visited. There had been many in the Woods family scattered around South China for many years, doing good work for Christianity and for the Chinese people. The good work referred to was in medical missions and the education of girls and Chinese church missions.

My parents and Dad's mother were also in the East at certain points. Anna Delaney, Dad's mother, took a long missionary trip, which took her to the Philippines in the late 1930s, and also to China. Also, Mother and Dad had become acquainted with Jiang Kai Shek and his wife, Mme. Song Mei Lin. I believe that this couple was trying to court favor with influential Americans, especially Christian leaders, and they were with my parents in that connection. They met at my parents' apartment in New York City, and my parents visited the Generalissimo and Mme. Jiang in Taipei in January 1957. They presented several gifts to my parents, including a framed picture of some of Mme. Jiang's ink drawings with a description of them and of her interest in art written by hand by him. That piece now hangs in our Charlottesville home.

Since that trip, I have traveled to China nine times in 1988, 1990–91, 1993, 1995, 1997, 1999, 2003, 2006, and 2008. Lydia and I were together on most of these trips, but some I took alone in a research effort for my book that I was planning on Christianity in China. In our travels, we have been to many places in China, in many regions from north to south and east to west, with the exception of the far northeastern provinces, in what has been called Manchuria.

Of particular importance to us was our year spent in Beijing from August 1990 to August 1991, when both Lydia and I taught in the Foreign Affairs College in Beijing. My experience of securing this job was interesting. I was on a bus in Beijing in 1988 by myself, when I turned to ask the Chinese man next to me where to get off at Peking University, now called Bei Da, or Beijing University. At the proper place, he got off and showed me where I wanted to go. Lydia and I came to call him Tom. We talked and decided to meet again. We became friends while we were there, with visits to his apartment with his wife and daughter. During the time of our first meeting at Bei Da, each of us told much about ourselves to each other.

I heard that he had communicated with a friend in the Foreign Affairs College, and one day, unexpectedly, I received a letter that came to my office at Longwood University, inviting me for a job as a "foreign expert" teaching at this famous college, whose mission it was to teach and to train diplomats and foreign-affairs workers in cities and institutions around China. To receive such an offer seemed, perhaps, like a marvelous coincidence—that is, if there really are any genuine coincidences in life. In my correspondence with this college, we secured a teaching position for Lydia. She was to teach English in speaking, writing, and reading. My position was that of a foreign expert in the field of what they called Western Political Philosophy.

We had a memorable and interesting time at Foreign Affairs College, teaching many students and absorbing the rich culture of the college and the city. Lydia taught first-year students English. One day, she found herself trying to help her Chinese students who found it difficult to distinguish between a "v" sound and that of a "w." She had them saying out loud, "Chairman Mao swam the wide river with vim, vigor, and vitality." Lydia also taught upper-level English studies, notably to an especially bright student named Zhou Fang. Zhou came to our apartment and showed how she learned to cook eggplant from her grandmother, using our wok and gas-burning small stove. Zhou Fang's paper was on selected writings of William Faulkner.

My main class was in political philosophy, and lo and behold, I found myself teaching the problem of civil disobedience in Beijing just a year and a few months after the Tiananmen Square Massacre, not too far from our college. I had these bright young people studying the principles of ethics and reading such philosophical greats as Plato, Aristotle, Locke, Hobbes, and John Rawls. Many of my students who were seniors or graduate students were very smart, well able to handle the speaking and the understanding of the English language in something as difficult and as abstract as philosophy.

One of the students in the class was missing, having been accused and arrested by the police, allegedly for starting a fire on a military vehicle just after what the Chinese called the Tiananmen "incident." This young man's account of his situation was that the military vehicle was already burning. His mother took him to the police station, where all was civil and respectful. When she left, everything changed for him, as he was treated harshly and sent away to prison. His name is Ye Jian.

His mother, whom we called Mrs. Guo, was a regular Communist Party member and loyal to the state and her position in a state college, under the Foreign Ministry. For a long time, she and her husband did not know where Ye Jian was or even whether he was alive or not. They were emotionally devastated. Mrs. Guo could not let down her guard with her coworkers, showing her true feelings about what the state had done to her son. However, she felt that she could let go emotionally with Lydia, with whom she was becoming a good friend. She cried out her tears in our apartment.

Later, she learned that Ye Jian was in a prison in the city of Tianjin, about two hours away from Beijing by train, and she learned that she could visit him. Mrs. Guo came to us one day asking if she could borrow $400 so that she could buy some things to bribe the guards, so that conditions would improve for her son in the prison. He had shown the authorities his intelligence and character and had become a translator at the jail in Tianjin. He had been given special quarters and good food to keep him healthy.

With his classmates, we were studying the topic of civil disobedience. One day, we wrote a letter from the class and sent it to Ye Jian through Mrs. Guo along with other papers the students had written on this subject. Mrs. Guo was smuggling papers on civil disobedience into the Chinese Tianjin jail! Soon we received a letter from the Tianjin jail from this supposedly civil disobedient prisoner, and we felt we had buttressed his spirits and strengthened his resolve.

Later, while we were on a trip to the far northwest in China, Lydia and I received a call from Mrs. Guo, who said there was someone she wanted us to talk to. It was Ye Jian, who had been freed in the early summer of 1991. What a celebration it was for Mrs. Guo and her son, for Ye Jian and his classmates—and also for me and Lydia! We had been part of something important.

Since a Chinese with a felony on his record could not secure work for any Chinese business, and since his rights were quite limited, Ye Jian chose to come to America. Lydia and I worked for him, helping him to get admitted to Marietta College in Ohio. At one point in this process, we wired $10,000 to the college so that he would have all his first-year expenses covered. This was a loan, not a gift, and both mother and son have repaid their loans to us. Ye Jian graduated and has become a computer specialist, working for companies in Chapel Hill, North Carolina. He got this job on his own. We still are connected with him even today.

Lydia and I made a life-enhancing discovery in Beijing after the first couple of months of our stay at Foreign Affairs College. Students and faculty saw that we didn't have an "ugly American" attitude toward the Chinese. They perceived that we were there to learn and to help educate students and that we had a "good attitude" about China. We were both experienced teachers, yet the degree of revelations and the opening up of these students to us personally in a heartfelt way was something new to us in our teaching careers.

One of my students, named Zou Xiaojie from Nanjing, China, invited me one night to go to a Chinese musical concert near our college. We have been friends ever since, and we visited each other many times. We became friends with her parents and with her American husband from Massachusetts, Steven Kohl. We spent much time together, until they left for her job in Hong Kong. Our telephone calls and e-mails are not as frequent as they used to be. We miss more constant contact with them.

Other special people among our students were Wang Jiwei, Xu Hongjian, Zhou Honglei, and Liu Wenyun. These bright and good people have meant so much to us over the years since 1990. We have seen them in China on visits after our year at Foreign Affairs College and have seen some of them in the United States. We have kept up with them pretty well since then. We have become friends with the father of Xu Hongjian and the parents of Wang Jiwei and Liu Wenyun. I have performed the wedding services of three of these people. First was the wedding of Zhou Honglei at our apartment in China. When I came to the appropriate moment to say that the groom may kiss the bride, Chinese custom led them to resist in following that suggestion out of modesty. I married Zou Xiaojie and Steven Kohl in a garden in St. Petersburg, Florida, and Liu Wenyun and her American husband at the Marble Collegiate Church in New York City.

We had to come home from our special, memorable year! Since that time, *I have become a Sinophile*—a lover of China. I live with a near constant sense of being absorbed in things Chinese. I also am becoming a China scholar. *My own personal becoming has been so influenced and enriched* over the years by my experiences with China and the Chinese. We have networks of Chinese friends and continuing contacts with certain Chinese institutions. We have befriended many people at the Drum Tower Hospital in Nanjing, China. We remember the good work of older members of Lydia's family, including her father and mother, in China. Out of our own experiences and with them in mind, we have set up a Peale-Woods Medical Scholarship, which has brought two young Chinese medical people, Shawn Soong and Xu Guomei, to the University of Virginia Medical Center for further training in their respective fields of hospital management and OR nursing. We are in the process now of bringing yet a third such medical person to the United States in 2012.

In 2005, I published my book on China, *The Love of God in China*, the subtitle of which is: *Can One Be Both Chinese and Christian?* The book was dedicated to Lydia, "who knows both what it means and what it meant." My goal in this volume was to make a contribution to the discussion of Christianity in China both here and in China, and I have succeeded in that goal. The book is not a best-seller—not like my dad's book, *The Power of Positive Thinking*—but it is out there for people to learn from and enjoy, and it can be ordered by searching the title on Amazon.com.

I have continued in my scholarly life to work out conclusions of certain issues and insights in that book. I have moved into another pattern of Chinese study also connected with that book. There is in me still a continuing passion about China and the Chinese. Most every day for many years, I have studied something about China, usually the language, current political situation, or its culture—and always its history. Wide and diverse reading about China has become an avocation for me. During my teaching career, people would see me walking around the campuses of my college, with my Walkman in my hand and ears, listening not to the latest sounds, but to the Chinese language. In Charlottesville, I am identified by many as a lover of China, and I offer no apology for that to anyone. In January 2012, I am not only sending this current book to the publisher, but I am presenting yet another scholarly paper on the concept of knowledge—Zhi Dao—to an academic meeting of the southeastern regional conference of the Association of Asian Studies at Furman University in Greenville, South Carolina. Quite recently, I have reconnected by e-mail with several of my former students at the Foreign Affairs College, some of whom are in the United States.

Chapter 13: Becoming in the Continued Quest for Knowledge and Insight

⁓

I n my adult life, after the completion of my formal studies in graduate schools and in the course of my teaching career, a main personal goal was to continue to gain and reflect knowledge and to achieve further insight. What I have been seeking is the ability to make a kind of intellectual penetration to the nub or essence or fundamentals of whatever the issue is—to get to the heart of the matter in question. Another way of saying this was suggested by a friend who liked to talk of reaching at least "the antechambers of truth." This is a purely intellectual task and a special kind of joy, in which I take personal delight.

I think back to my teachers who had done what I still want to do, beginning first with Edwin Myers at Washington and Lee. His was a powerful intellect. He, together with James Layburn, was the man who first set me on the intellectual road toward greater understanding. I used to go to see him in his office about some matter in my studies in philosophy. He was always hunched over his book in his easy chair—a model of concentration. When interrupting him as a young student, I was usually breaking out in a cold sweat.

I also wanted to be like David Falk, professor of philosophy at the University of North Carolina at Chapel Hill. He penetrated to the heart of the philosophy of David Hume, with subtle and profound understanding and insight. I have succeeded also in becoming like him, including in his care for students with whom he was working. I recall once when I was teaching courses on Hume, I could feel the power of Falk in my mind and heart as I, too, penetrated to the heart of his philosophy in both my papers and my teaching. Students were writing an exam on Hume, all thinking about Hume. My comment then was that the exam was "humorous."

I have become proud as the years have gone by that often I can and many times do think clearly enough to penetrate to the heart of the intellectual matter before me. This gives me immense satisfaction. It has been a profoundly important factor in my personal development. I believe that I have done this through understanding the Chinese and China, especially in my understanding of Christianity and the native Chinese philosophies, which I am continuing to study and learn even at the time of this writing. I recall once being the subject of that particular kind of Chinese criticism, which praised my work, including with the sentence that I was at least half Chinese. I took this as a distinct compliment.

In my later years of reading and discussing matters of interest, I attempt further cultivation of this type of ability. A couple of years ago, I sought to understand the position in theology and social ethics of Reinhold Niebuhr. Partly, I was stimulated to do this in a very delayed reaction to the letter quoted above that my father wrote to me saying that he and Reinhold Niebuhr were "implacable" enemies. I carefully studied several major works of Niebuhr's, such as the two-volume work entitled *The Nature and Destiny of Man*. I team-taught an adult education class at my church with another theologian and friend, Owen Norment. I came to clearly see what he meant, but also that the implacability was not necessarily so.

Currently, I continue to probe the fascinating character of T. E. Lawrence, known as "Lawrence of Arabia." There are so many interesting issues about him and his life, the force of his will leading him to make an immense contribution to the Arab uprising and conquest of Aqaba around the time of WWI. It is troubling to see his intellectual and willful heroic exploits and yet to see his taking on two pseudonyms later in life as he sought anonymity in different branches of the British military, yet also working on his highly important work, The *Seven Pillars of Wisdom*. All at once, he was becoming famous through that work and becoming anonymous and hidden in his life, which lasted not long until his motorcycle accident in which he died. The role of my former acquaintance, Lowell Thomas, was interesting in all of this, and interesting biographies have been written to understand this man and his life. These kind of intellectual quests are largely the stuff of my life in "retirement."

In the early 1990s, I felt secure enough in my understanding and learning to take on another task, that of explaining positive thinking to Mother and Dad and their associates at Guideposts. I wanted to show them that I not only understood positive thinking, but also supported this point of view, even if I still had my critical issues with it. I wanted Dad and Mother to see that I felt much more sympathy and loyalty than perhaps they understood of me.

Interlude 2:
What Is the Power of
Positive Thinking?

G uideposts holds meetings of its National Advisory Cabinet regularly at different locations in the country, and this meeting was part of that regular pattern. What was not part of a regular pattern was what was going on in me as I prepared for this meeting. I decided that I was going to have a special mission here—to show my parents that I understood positive thinking and supported it as a way of thinking that can be helpful to people. I also wanted to show the Guideposts staff a more complete understanding of the philosophy of my dad.

It needs to be understood that my parents thought that I had strayed away into academia and therefore wasn't in full support of the virtues of positive thinking. They had good reason to think this, I guess. But I had good reason to want to let them know, particularly my dad who was nearing the end of his life, how I felt. I wanted them to understand that even with what they saw as my "straying away" and in spite of the way that he had personally backed off from me, that after all this, I understood and loved them and supported the point of view of positive thinking. I was going to show them something that I hoped would be special for them.

My father's health was becoming more of a problem in this last year before he passed away. It was to be the year of his final public speech in the fall of 1992 that he was to give at his alma mater, Ohio

Wesleyan University in Delaware, Ohio. This was the time, I thought, to give him a present of my understanding and support. Most likely, a sense that he lacked my support had been in his mind and heart all the years before.

Speech I gave at Loews L'Enfant Hotel in Washington, DC, titled "The Abundant Life," at a meeting of the National Advisory Cabinet of Guideposts, on September 28, 1992

❝ I am here this afternoon to talk with you about something near and dear to our hearts. I want us to think together about the abundant life. We all care about the quality of our lives. In many ways, we do many things to improve and upgrade this quality. The abundant life is something we all want and all strive for; it is something I expect many of us here present have known.

"There is a principle well established in religion and in science, a principle my father came to call the power of positive thinking. I am here to affirm this principle and to proclaim it to the world. This principle is firmly rooted in the Christian faith.

"Positive thinkers, as I understand them, believe in the life-changing presence of Jesus Christ in their lives. Positive thinkers are Christians who believe in God, who go to church and have fellowship with other Christians, and who try to apply their faith to their everyday lives. For positive thinkers, Jesus the Christ is a reality which enters our lives and changes us. By practicing positive thinking and by accepting the lifesaving and enhancing presence of the Lord Jesus Christ in our lives, we all can have the abundant life.

"My father and my mother, both of whom I love dearly, have been preaching and practicing these principles most all their lives. They have ministered to millions. Through a wonderful combination in them as a team, of creativity, administrative ability, and hard work, they have created a message; they have sustained a wonderful organization to carry on their work, to continue to communicate the message. You all believe in and support this organization, now called the Peale Center for Christian Living. I am fifty-six years old now, but not old enough to remember its birth. I do remember sitting around our dining room table long ago and stuffing Dad's sermons into envelopes, so that they could be sent out to the list of contributors to Sermon Publications Inc. I am a member of the board of trustees of the Peale Center and am active on many of its programs. I am here today to give my version of the message, and to declare that the talented and dedicated staff of the Peale Center, the entire Peale biological family and larger Peale Center family, which includes you all, will continue to spread this positive message to our needy and troubled world.

"Of course, my father has been declaring the message of positive thinking for a long time. We all know that he has done a lot of good for lots of people. Or so it seems. He has told a great story about how much good he did for one person in California some years ago.

"'A number of years ago, I was having dinner one night with some friends in a dim-lit swanky, sophisticated restaurant in Hollywood, California, known as the Brown Derby. (I was told that this was no place for a preacher, but I always pick up on a free meal wherever one is available.) We were sitting to the rear of this restaurant in a booth, having a delightful time, when I suddenly became aware of the fact that there was in the restaurant a hitherto unknown friend of mine I'd never met before.

"'He seemed to have some interest in me, and if he'd ever had any reticence, he had a long since been separated from it. He was walking around this restaurant crying out in raucous and strident tones so that all might hear, "Where's Dr. Peale?"

"'Well, friends,' Dad says, 'I'm no shrinking violet, but I did not particularly care for this form of publicity, and I shrank down in my booth trying to render myself inconspicuous. But apparently, men afflicted as he was have a kind of unerring perceptiveness, and presently he located me. He came and leaned down over me, bringing close up against me a thin, watery, bloodshot eye, and asked, "Are you Dr. Peale?" I admitted my identity, whereupon he put out his hand in kind of jocular fashion and said, "Well, put'er there, boy! I've read all of your books. You've done me an awful lot of good."

"'With that, he disappeared.'

"Years later, Dad received this letter:

Dear Dr. Peale:

About fifteen years ago you were in the Brown Derby Restaurant in Hollywood, California, when a very drunk young man invaded your dinner party to compliment you on your books. He told you how much your books had helped him.

A few years later you were speaking in Dallas, Texas, at a big dinner affair. Your opening joke was about the actual knowledge you had of your writings having been of assistance to people, or at least to one person. You then told how this drunk young man accosted you and placed his cold, clammy hand in yours and stated, "Dr. Peale, I've read every one of your books and, man, they've really helped me.

I was the only one there in the front row or any other row that night who knew that your story was true, since I was the person you were talking about. But my life has been changed by Jesus Christ. I'm a new man now. In fact, I'm a Mormon, and you know the Mormon attitude towards whiskey, tobacco, even coffee and tea; and I have strictly adhered to it. So maybe your book really helped me some after all.

"Dad adds: 'That is a story of the resurrection from the dead of a broken, defeated personality through the power of Jesus Christ, who is in everybody's life and is forever new.

"'Have faith in Christ. Live with Christ. Make your life immortal through Christ. And never be afraid of either love or death.'

"The principle behind the power of positive thinking is an old idea, at least as old as Epictetus, the stoic philosopher, and Marcus Aurelius, the most philosophical of Roman Emperors. Yet it is new and fresh and creative, when we apply it to our lives.

"We human beings are constantly thinking evaluative thoughts about ourselves and our lives. We are often our own severest critics and judges of our lives and how we're living them. Many of our feelings, emotions, and attitudes about ourselves are based on these thoughts. These thoughts about ourselves may be accurate or inaccurate, positive or negative. Troubles come when disturbed feelings arise from them. Worries, anxieties, doubts sometimes flood our consciousness. When our thoughts about ourselves are inaccurate or negative, these negative feelings are made more intense and troubling to us, and we have personal problems.

"Another principle in the power of positive thinking is that we human beings have a power over our thoughts. The power over our thoughts gives us power over our feelings and emotions. There are times when we cannot directly control the way we feel, as anxieties or fears simply sweep over us. But we human beings have a tool to control these seemingly uncontrollable desires and emotions, and that power is the power of thought. We have the power to set aside our personal unreflective feelings and inclinations and to think clearly and crisply about what we're like and what we should do.

"We can inquire whether our reflections about ourselves are accurate or not. We can do this ourselves or we can get the counsel of someone else who might have a clearer perception of us. We also can set aside negative thoughts about ourselves and replace them with positive thoughts about our abilities and capacities.

"Out of this process of thinking and feeling about ourselves, we all develop a self-image. No one should ever underestimate the power of self-esteem and self-image over our lives. Our image of ourselves colors everything we do, and it leads us to act the way we do.

"There is another principle built into the power of positive thinking. It is this: we become the kind of person that fits our self-image. By the power of our thought, we can develop a self-image that is positive and accurate, and we can concentrate on that, fixing that in our minds. If we exercise the power of thought to project a positive self-image, then we will become positive persons.

"By practicing the power of positive thinking, I say that we can even change our state of life by changing our states of mind. That claim was first asserted and argued by William James about 1910.

"Now I am a college professor, what is known in the trade as a 'full' professor, in my case a full professor of philosophy. I never quite understood why university or college professors are called 'full' professors. Perhaps it's because we are full of ourselves or full of it, as they say. Anyway, I was highly influenced by my major professor in college, Dr. Edwin Myers. I always wanted to be like he was, and I guess I've done that. Myers had a sterling reputation on our campus when I was in college. I hope each of you had your Dr. Myers. The memorable influence of a great professor on the mind of a college-aged young person can be a powerful influence on a person's life. Dr. Myers was a philosopher king for me.

"That reminds me of something. As a professor, I have a colleague named David Stein, a psychologist, who told me something interestingly recently. 'It is my belief that your dad introduced the first ideas that lead to the development of a theory of personality and treatment methods known as cognitive restructuring. Generally Albert Ellis is credited as the first modern day writer on this subject. In reality, your dad got there first. The main idea in this approach is that thoughts (cognitions) precede emotions. We can learn to control our emotions by learning to control our thoughts. Your dad pointed out the importance of this concept.'

"David Stein, himself a cognitive restructuralist, is talking about the power of positive thinking.

"My own career as a professor has lasted about twenty years to date. I have remembrances of many young people who have passed through my classrooms, my office, my home, and my life. Many of these students have been bright and eager; some have been sluggish and uncaring, not knowing really why they were in college. A few of them I will never forget, for they have left a powerful influence for good in my life.

"I'd like to tell you about one of these students. He was a person who learned how to practice the power of positive thinking in the face of an extremely challenging and difficult situation.

"His name was James Scott. I regret that I've lost touch with him in the last few years. He came to our college originally to play football, having been recruited as a linesman for the position of tackle. He was a black student, big and strong and quick on his feet.

"At the beginning of his sophomore year, he decided that he didn't want to play football anymore. Some skeptics said he wouldn't be making the team in his second year, but I didn't know about that. I got to know him after his decision about leaving football, when he said that he wanted to change his life to become a student. I got to know him in the fall of that sophomore year, when he came into my office to tell me that he wanted to major in religion and philosophy.

"Now this is good news for a professor of philosophy, especially to this professor who is religious and who is interested in religion as an academic subject. The trouble was that, according to standard measurements, James was not very well prepared for college. His high school grades were poor to medium, his SAT scores were low, and his college grades during his first year came to a D average.

"As time went on, we got to know each other. He was in two of my courses that fall. He told me that he was a Christian, that he had an active church life and a prayer life, and that his father was a Baptist preacher. In his senior year, I had the occasion to go to his father's church and to hear his father preach. Those of you who have had a similar experience know that real black Baptist preachers really preach with a high energy level, and the spirit really is alive and rocking in their churches. Compared to them, we white preachers just talk.

"In that sophomore fall semester, trouble started brewing for James about the time for the first test. I am happy to report that Professor Peale always has had a reputation among students for giving tests that make significant demands on students. They are hard tests, and good grades on them don't come easily, even though Professor Peale tempers justice with mercy. All this worried James, and he came to me asking for extra time to talk about the ideas and to practice writing.

"James needed such practice. He really didn't know how to talk about abstract ideas; he could hardly write a decent English sentence. He had almost no classroom background in the subject. Most importantly, he didn't have much confidence that he could take and pass this test. His self-image as a student was low and shaky.

"But he came to my office over and over again, almost every evening until well past my normal bedtime. He pestered the heck out of this professor, but in his case, I accepted and even looked forward to his interruptions of my own work and life. Something important was going on in this boy's struggle to change the way he had always thought about himself as a student.

"During our evening meetings, we wrote sentences together, and he rewrote them; we talked about the material in the class, and we reviewed it. On some few occasions, he was so frustrated that he even cried and expressed his personal bad and confused feelings over his inabilities and confusions. Several times, we prayed together to God, asking that even in these troubling times for him, he would know the peace of God in his life, so that he could work his hardest and to his best.

"He got a D grade on the first test, and he was really discouraged. I encouraged him. I helped him rewrite the test, phrase by phrase. He rewrote that first test four times, until he had it where I could have given him a B grade. On the second test, he had improved his grade to a low C. We went through the same procedures with Test II.

"Gradually, with lots of hard work and encouragement and gentle but probing criticism, I could see in him and viscerally feel in him, the beginnings of a change in his own estimate of himself as a student. Positive thoughts were finding their way into the troubled self-consciousness and low self-esteem of James Scott. He had another crisis of confidence in his worry and anxiety about the final exam. I let him postpone the term paper until he had more time in the summer.

"We worked and struggled together on that final exam, and I was immensely proud and happy to read the test and be able to put a grade of B on it. Over the summer, he produced a paper good enough for him to earn a B- grade for the course.

"I was happy again to see him return in the fall with a light in his eye and a spring in his step and the kind of good humor and jocularity which comes to a student, or to any person in any field, who is gaining confidence in his abilities in his work.

"His parents came to his graduation, and together with this proud professor, they watched him walk across the platform, past the faculty sitting in our academic regalia. He shook hands with the president of the college, took his degree from the vice-president for Academic Affairs, and walked into the crowd to give his Mom a big bear hug. Later, she gave me a big hug with tears in her eyes. There were tears of appreciation in the eyes of his father, the Baptist preacher.

"James Scott had graduated as a major in religion and philosophy. In our close times together, I had literally watched him become educated. He was a different person in his speaking, his writing, and thinking, and especially in his healthy self-image and self-confidence. That is a wonderful thing for people in my profession to see. James Scott became educated because he practiced the power of positive thinking, to put behind him his negative self-image as a student and to concentrate on a developing sense of confidence built up over three years of hard work.

"James Scott had entered into the abundant life.

"In the Gospel of John at the 10th chapter, verse 10, we read that Jesus says that he came that we might have life and have it more abundantly.

"Perhaps many of you know that this text was the first text on which my father preached years ago, and I would offer the prediction that, if he knew when his last sermon would be preached, this would also be his text on that occasion.

"A person enters the abundant life fully when that person allows Jesus Christ to enter his life. For Jesus Christ to enter our lives, we have to offer ourselves to him, surrendering our preoccupation with our own sense of ego, our own sense that we are in complete control of our lives.

"The truth is that we are not in complete control of our lives, for we have negative feelings and troubling personal states which sometimes dominate our lives. We can become dominated by worries, anxieties, and bad feelings.

"James Scott had grown up and come up in school for many years with the belief that he was a poor student. He hated that and tried to escape the problem by finding a way to succeed personally through playing football. He always had self-confidence in his football ability.

"When he was struggling to be a student, he and I talked about how he could become one if he worked hard and thought of himself as a good student. In his condition, that was very hard for him to do. James Scott needed help.

"He found that help in the power of faith in Jesus Christ. He let Jesus Christ back into his life, surrendering himself again to his Master, as his father and mother had taught him to do. When he did that, he received what I like to call an enabling grace. When the spirit of Christ was in his heart, he had a freedom from the heavy feelings of inferiority and inability, a freedom to study and concentrate and work on his writing and reading and speaking and thinking.

"With the spirit of Christ in his heart, he had a peace of mind which gave him the freedom from worries and anxieties. By giving him this peace, by giving him this enabling grace, God was giving James Scott the conditions in which he could practice the power he had in him to set aside his worries and anxieties and to think positive thoughts about being a good student. And he could concentrate on a positive self-image as a student. He had to work hard at this. No one has ever said that practicing the power of positive thinking over negative feelings and emotions is easy.

"James had the peace of Christ and God's enabling grace in him. His parents, his teachers, his friends gave him encouragement. He became what he projected as his positive self-image, a good student undergraduate major in his chosen field. With Paul, he could say, 'I can do all things in Him who strengthens me.'

"What I have told about James Scott can apply to each one of us in our own daily struggles in life. We too can use the tool of the power in our thinking to control the debilitating influence of anxieties and worries. We too can allow Jesus the Christ into our lives, surrendering ourselves to him. From the presence of the living Christ in our hearts, we will be at peace no matter how difficult the situation, and we will know his enabling grace.

"The staff of the Peale Center for Christian Living, and the Peale family, following the blessed examples of Norman Vincent and Ruth Stafford Peale, believe in this message of a positive Christian faith. We're dedicated to getting this positive message out to the world in the most powerful and effective ways possible.

"We are enjoying the strong support of you members of the National Advisory Cabinet and you donors to the Peale Center. Your support and counsel helps to comfort and strengthen us for the task ahead.

"God bless you, every one."

As I was making my speech, I was attempting to set forth as clearly and as forcefully as I could Dad's view of positive thinking and to show how powerful it can be in human lives. I feel like I talked with power and sincerity, and so people believed.

As I was presenting my speech, I noticed something really unusual, which was the look on the face of my mother. It seemed that she was in a kind of surprise and pleasure, with a dropped jaw indicating a shock over what she was hearing. Out of the corner of my eye, I could see her making a gesture to an executive of the Peale Center for Christian Living, Eric Fellman. She was letting Eric know of her good feelings about the speech and of me, in such a pleasant surprise and over what was so unexpected. Upon seeing this, I knew that I was getting through to her.

After the speech, Dad was mixing in the lobby of the hotel with other people. As he was going up to his room in the elevator, he bragged proudly and with obvious pleasure that this was the best speech on positive thinking that he had ever heard. Perhaps he didn't, at that time, remember the many excellent speeches he had given himself on this topic.

My mission seemed to have become fulfilled. I was happy about that, but there was in me still that gap between what I did and what I really felt in my heart. I felt that this was just another try to get close to him, to reestablish the close personal contact that we had before my high school years and before Dad became famous.

Chapter 14: Becoming in Marriage and Family

Life was good for me and Lydia, and made better, certainly different, with the birth of our first child. This came while we were living in New York City during my third year at Union Theological Seminary. Life was never the same after that.

In the wee hours of October 30, 1962, I went out into the streets of New York and hailed a cab, and we were taken quickly to the Cornell Medical Center on the East River, where only after a little time, Lydia gave birth to our first child, Laura Stafford Peale. We will never forget how different things were after we brought her back to our living quarters at Union Seminary. What I remember most were those bright blue eyes.

There is an interesting story of the birth of our second child. I was studying then in Chicago, looking to start my teaching career in 1967, when our son was born. It happened that Lydia went to the Michael Reese Hospital, and her labor pains stopped, and she was then admitted into the hospital. When the pains started up again more seriously, she was rushed to delivery. Meanwhile, I had gone home to our Hyde Park condominium home and was sound asleep.

I was called at 1:11 a.m. and informed that we had a newborn son, whom we named Charles Clifford Peale, the same name as my dad's dad, whom I had looked up to so much when I was a boy. I saw us continuing a family tradition.

Our third child was born two years later on May 24, 1967, and we named her Sarah Lacy Peale. It was a normal, easy, and quick delivery, and Lydia's parents were there to welcome the new baby. We thought we might name the newborn Margaret Lacy, the Margaret being for my older sister. However, I chose Sarah as the first name, and Lydia accepted this. The beautiful thing was that we had another baby in the family. Lacy had a big shock of black hair, which she quickly lost, and Lydia really enjoyed the one-week hospital rest provided by our medical insurance at that time.

Our early family life was happy and active as I was getting started on my chosen academic career. After a memorable and successful three-year tenure at Elmhurst, we headed for my chosen university where I was to seek and gain my PhD. It has been good for us to remember that we left Chicago two weeks before the Democratic National Convention, the one in which Abraham Ribicoff challenged Mayor Daley, speaking from the podium about "police state tactics" of the Chicago Police Department. His words were clear, but those of Daley shouting red-faced from the audience, appropriately, were not. There were protests in neighboring Grant Park, the same place in which Barack Obama gave his rousing speech after being elected president of the United States.

We moved to Blue Heaven, otherwise known as Chapel Hill, North Carolina, home of the University of North Carolina and the Tar Heel basketball team. We moved into a small three-bedroom home. Soon after, we got a beagle puppy, which we named Samuel, the same name as the father of my grandfather. For some time, our oldest child, Laura, was scared of the dog—until one evening she managed to go into the fenced backyard and be with the dog, who came up to her. Laura first backed off with anxiety, but then she got up courage and put her arms around him, and that was the end of a family problem. It was very sad later that Samuel got glaucoma and began to bump into furniture in the house. One day, he got out and was struck and killed by a passing car. It was a sad moment indeed when we took Samuel's body to the local vet, who had the dog buried. After Samuel, we had yet another beagle puppy named Janet.

Our life in Chapel Hill was active, fun, interesting, and close. I blossomed in my studies at the university, and our family grew together. One thing that drew us together was that we all became strong fans of the UNC men's basketball team. One special time early on came when we all were watching the team when Charlie Scott made a shot from the top of the key, which produced string music and was enough to beat Davidson in the finals of the East Regional in the NCAA tournament. It was a memorable event for all of us.

In something of an unusual event, my parents came to visit us one Christmas, and the memories of this visit are still pleasant. We had such a good time, which meant lots to me, but still there was the other side of the coin, as I realized yet again the nagging separation between me and Dad. I don't remember any attention, interest, or encouragement from him in my graduate studies there.

From Chapel Hill, we moved to Danville, Virginia, where I had a teaching job at Stratford College while I was finishing my degree. We lived on Westmoreland Court, just minutes from the college and also from where all of our children were in school, with Lacy starting kindergarten.

Laura was a little girl with bright eyes and big glasses who loved to read. The librarian of the school, Mrs. Hillsheimer, loved children who loved books. Years later after Laura had earned her Library Science degree at Simmons College in Boston, she also landed what was her second job at the famed Boston Public Library. The next day, I telephoned Mrs. Hillsheimer and asked if she was in a seated position. Then I proudly told her that the little girl with the big glasses just got a big job as a librarian at the Boston Public Library. Mrs. Hillsheimer said that she felt chills running up and down her spine!

We moved from Danville to Chatham, Virginia, and I continued in my work as a professor. Our lives were fun during these years, as the kids enjoyed being at a school that was, for them, like a country club—with all sorts of opportunities for children of a faculty member to raise hell and get away with it.

With Clifford, I engaged in an activity with other sons and fathers who were making and competing in races in what we called the Pinewood Derby. Sons and fathers made wooden cars that raced along tracks to a finish line. The competition was keen. In our first try, Cliff and I did not take it seriously, which we discovered was a big mistake. Our car came in dead last, and we received no points. There was nothing to recognize the last-place car. The next go around, we both made serious attempts to have an especially sleek and fine car. We placed third, and our feelings were assuaged somewhat. At least we got the last-place monkey off our back.

We moved from Chatham to Farmville, Virginia, where I had secured a position at Longwood College, now Longwood University, where I eventually taught for twenty-three years before retiring in 1999. I enjoyed my teaching career at Longwood, as I have described in my section on becoming in my teaching career.

I remember one incident in Farmville when I visited Lacy in her grade school class. I told of her being mystified by the bowl of warm water with a piece of lemon in it put on our table after dinner. In those days, there were such bowls given in some restaurants, called a "finger bowl." Such bowls of warm water were given so that diners could effectively clean their hands between courses. Not knowing what to do with it, Lacy picked up the bowl and began drinking the water! She had to endure the joking she received from my telling of this, as I did tell so many stories about the children as they were growing up, sometimes to their embarrassment. They knew, I believe, that love was coming through.

We were engaged actively in our life in Farmville for a long time, with Lydia teaching in the Prince Edward County High School. I was teaching at Longwood College. We were active in church life at the College Church at the nearby Hampden-Sydney College.

Lydia and I were active in Farmville and Virginia politics, as members of the local Democratic Committee and hosting a significant number of events of political importance as we promoted democratic candidates for state and national offices.

Work in Race Relations

One of the things I am proud of for our family is our involvement in race relations between whites and blacks in various places we have lived. This was particularly true in Prince Edward County, which had been the scene of the closing of the public schools from 1959 to 1964. It had become one of the five cases before the Supreme Court of the United States in *Brown vs. the Board of Education* in 1954. This kind of activity in Farmville set us in a liberal mode, seeking to change the customs of society relative to race relations for the better.

In Farmville, we were associated with the culture at the predominately black Prince Edward County High School, where Lydia taught and each of our three children went to school. Through this association, we actively promoted more open race relations. For example, after we arrived, we found that there was no established social setting in which black and white children could mingle openly. So we and other liberally minded families opened our homes to have parties. We lived on a main street where established families lived, and parties we gave were open, and we "suffered" some negative reaction for the type of parties we were hosting.

We came to learn about relations from the inside out in this community where the history of the school closings forced the issue right out into the open. Our children went to school with black friends and loved it and learned so much from it. At Prince Edward High School, each of our children found meaning in life by cultivating creative and harmonious race relations. When they went on to college, they continued their understanding in their studies. Our oldest child, Laura, at Kenyon College in Ohio, wrote her senior paper in her major in religion on the black Muslim movement. Our middle child, Cliff, at Williams College in Massachusetts, wrote his major paper in political science on the legal antecedents of the *Brown vs. Board of Education* Supreme Court case. Our youngest child, Lacy, at Dickinson College in Pennsylvania, wrote her major paper in American studies on specific works of the black writer Toni Morrison.

Lydia and I continued to work to promote good race relations with Lydia's teaching black and white children at high school and my work serving as secretary treasurer of the McGovern-Shriver Campaign Committee in the county in 1972. Also, I was a leader in the campaign of a local black candidate for mayor of Farmville against a white establishment candidate while I was a professor at Longwood College. We read much about the history of race relations in our county, and we became involved in democratic-oriented activities in our town and county for racial openness and change. Everyone in our family is proud of this sort of social-political commitment. Such openness and political and social liberality has been our way wherever we have lived.

In Farmville, we were a happy family, most of the time united in mutual love and respect. For example, I was proud to become an afterthought in the minds of many citizens of Farmville, who referred to me as the husband of Lydia or the father of our children. We were active in the affairs of my college, through student organizations and interesting events, some of which were in our family "required cultural events" for our three children.

It was in 1994 that we sensed the need to make a move, and we came to live in Fluvanna County in a residential community in the woods called Lake Monticello. We resided there for fourteen years before moving to our current location in our McGuffey Hill condominium unit in downtown Charlottesville, were we have lived since 2009.

Chapter 15: Becoming in My Church Life

Marble Collegiate Church

One of the ways in which I have been influenced by both my parents, but especially my dad, is in my church life. This influence goes back to when I was a boy sitting in the pastor's pew with my mother and my sisters at Marble Collegiate Church. With considerable emotion and pride, I would look up at and to my father as he preached or prayed in public, admiration and love filling my heart. How proud I was.

This church was noted for its friendliness and openness in the city of New York. Although it did not advertise itself as such, it was just as open and inclusive as other churches that proclaimed these characteristics loudly and obviously. A warm sanctuary seating about twelve hundred people was decorated in dark red carpets and pew covers. The front of the church was ornamented with gilded columns and a large pointed archway over and around the choir loft, just behind the raised platform-pulpit.

The congregation was blessed with a talented musical staff, with a professional organist and lead singers and an impressive musical complement to the service. The liturgy was both dignified and informal, befitting the character of the senior minister, my dad. My sisters and I grew up in this church and remember with great pleasure the special times we had there, which included baptisms and receiving the gilded leather-bound Bibles given to us upon our confirmation into the church. Special services there included my ordination service, my sister Maggie's wedding service, and numerous times we participated in special services of recognition for our father, particularly the "Celebration of the Life of NVP" service for him on December 29, 1993, just after his death. The church is part of the Collegiate Church in the City of New York in the Dutch Reformed Church denomination. It was at Marble where I was ordained in 1965, with my father giving the charge at that service.

Other Churches Where We Lived

Everywhere I have gone to school and lived, there have been churches that I attended. It cannot be emphasized too strongly how much of an influence my church life at and after Marble meant to my personal development and becoming.

Other churches included the Deerfield Church in Massachusetts, the Lexington, Virginia, Presbyterian Church, the Harvard Chapel, the Berkeley, Rhode Island, Methodist Church, James Chapel at Union Seminary in New York City, the Hyde Park Methodist Church in Chicago, the Presbyterian Church of Reconciliation in Chapel Hill, the First Presbyterian Church in Danville, the Chatham Virginia Presbyterian Church, the College Church at Hampden-Sydney, and the Westminster Presbyterian Church in Charlottesville.

In some of these churches, our family attended regularly and participated minimally in the life of the congregation. Our presence there on a regular basis, however, was important to us. In some of these churches, Lydia and I and the children became quite involved. In these churches, my religious life and my witness was becoming active in the church fellowship, always with a palpable sense of worship. In some cases, I became involved in work in justice and peace issues in our increasingly complex world. It is these few churches that I will emphasize in what follows.

In the Lexington Presbyterian Church, I was involved in Westminster Christian Fellowship and the ecumenical movement of our church with other churches in the area. We organized and attended conferences that worked on the cutting edge of this new interchurch movement, which was just beginning in American Christianity at the time. Also at this church, I was very much a part of a Friday afternoon informal and regular theological and social action student discussion group. We talked about issues of the day with substantial friends and student colleagues at Washington and Lee University. These discussions would set the stage for my active, intelligent participation in liberal circles of the day.

Since 1971, while I have lived in Virginia, I have been "on call" to preach in Presbyterian churches and to lead in weddings and other kinds of services. In this connection, I have been under the care of the Classis of New York in the Reformed Church in America, making annual reports of all my church activities up to retirement.

While I was in Boston, it was at the Harvard Chapel that I heard and learned so much about the best in preaching under the influence of Rev. George Buttrick, chaplain of Harvard College at that time. Of course, I had learned much about the very best preaching of the day under my own father and was always extremely proud of that. I also appreciated the talents and the various homiletical virtues of other fine preachers. Two of these were Reinhold Niebuhr and Paul Tillich. It was while I was at Union Theological Seminary that I worked under another great preacher named David H. C. Reid of the Madison Avenue Presbyterian Church in New York.

It was from the Harvard Chapel that Lydia would write me notes on the sermons of George Buttrick, which I would use indirectly in my first pastorate of my own ministry at the Berkeley Methodist Church. It was while I was at Union that I learned a valuable lesson from one of the greatest preachers of the time, Edmund Steimle. He was professor of homiletics at Union, and in his classes, he told the story of his own experiment with preaching under the inspiration of the Holy Spirit. In one instance, he decided that he would not work in the usual way in his study to prepare his sermon, but would be in prayer for the inspiration of the Holy Spirit in his life. That inspiration finally came on strong to him as he entered the pulpit to preach on the given Sunday. The Holy Spirit said to him at that moment: "Steimle, you're lazy!"

At the Church of Reconciliation at Chapel Hill, our family was engaged in this congregation in a most significant way. When we lived in Chapel Hill, I served this church for a time as its minister. This was something of an experimental church that met in the cafeteria of the Guy B. Philips Junior High School, where we had piano or guitar musical accompaniment. It was in the middle of the church service, after the sermon, that we would gather as a congregation to discuss the issues of the day. We had a "Church House" at the interface of the black and white communities in Chapel Hill where we centered our efforts in church work in racial reconciliation in that place.

It has been at our Westminster Presbyterian Church in Charlottesville that we have come to more mature and deeply active work in the church and in the world in the name of the church. Lydia has been singing in the choir and has been working on the Session, on committees on the church library, and fundraising for youth pilgrimage trips. I have been on the Adult Education Committee and on the Organ Concert Board. Our church, with our participation, engages with other churches in a PACEM program—"people and congregations engaged in ministry." We take in some forty homeless men on a two-week basis each year to help in ministry to that population.

I am one of the local leaders of a group called Clergy and Laity United for Justice and Peace in Central Virginia. We engage the church in political and social justice in our area. This year, we have had a series of programs beginning two days after the tenth anniversary of 9/11/01. We considered the topic of vengeance or revenge, following lines of thought in the rich and stimulating book by Gerald G. May entitled *Will and Spirit.* We have had an interfaith emphasis in our considerations of this topic, having speakers and discussions led by Christian, Muslim, and Jewish leaders and academicians. We will be reaching out later this spring of 2012 with a community organization called Impact, composed of more than thirty congregations and faith communities in our area to reach out the work of the church into the world. The leading issue this year is job readiness for young adults under thirty years of age.

Chapter 16: Becoming in Living with Serious Health Problems

$\backsim m \sim$

I never really compared myself to my dad in matters of physical health. This issue was not a threat or a sensitive matter between us. As I think back about him, I can see that he was a healthy man, as I never remember any serious problems for him until the near the end of his long and active life. Interestingly, my own children have many memories of a healthy Dad prior to my recent health problems. I am old enough, however, to appreciate one thing Dad said about his physical health when he was getting older and was beginning to have some difficulty getting around. He said, "The legs go first."

Like me, and perhaps all Peale males, he had a weight problem. In his middle years, he grew very heavy through the middle. I never knew how many pounds he hit on the scale. In his older years, he had lost much of this weight and had adjusted his weight to suit his physical height of about five feet eight inches. My weight went up when I was in my fifties and sixties, but now it has lowered considerably to go along better with my height, about five feet nine inches.

In my early years, I was a healthy boy going through the usual scrapes and accidents. One time, I almost cut off my right earlobe as I dove across Dad's study, cracking my head against a corner of his desk. I had been making like Captain Midnight, of one of my favorite old-time, late-afternoon radio programs. In school, I had my share of sports-related injuries. I do not remember when I broke my first bone, but I vividly remember dislocating my left shoulder as a young adult. This occurred in Danville, Virginia, when I was riding a bicycle down a hill on pavement when suddenly I flew over the handlebars of my bike and slammed my shoulder into the street. The nut attaching the handlebars to the body of the bike had come loose, and over I had gone. Laura, who was then just twelve years old, was with me. She was scared by the incident but coolly walked with me to the hospital. This was a problem I lived with, having several additional painful dislocations until I had an operation later on.

In the late 1960s, when we lived in Chapel Hill, I had a serious gall bladder operation. In Chapel Hill's Memorial Hospital, I remember almost dying one night in 1969. I had been having pains in my upper stomach and lower chest cavity, and my doctors were puzzled. One Sunday morning after Lydia had gone to church, I couldn't stand the pain and checked myself into the hospital. I was diagnosed as having an acute gallbladder attack with a blocked common duct, with peritonitis, a serious inflammation. I was admitted to the hospital, and later, Lydia came to be with me. That night, I had an operation that lasted six hours. Before saying good night, Lydia and I half-joked by saying to each other, "See you in the morning, darling," this after a famous exchange between Peter and Catherine Marshall on the night of Peter's death. Peter Marshall had been a noted minister of the New York Avenue Presbyterian Church in Washington, DC.

When the surgeon, Dr. Stanley Mandel, came out of the operating room to see Lydia, he said something like this: "His vital signs are good; he *may* make it." Unbeknownst to me, Dr. Mandel had called my parents in the middle of the night, and a couple of days later, they showed up to see me in intensive care. I looked at them through the haze of Demerol and other drugs. They looked so good and, I remember somehow, incredibly neat. They were loving to me and concerned and relieved that I was still breathing. It was a moment of closeness, though I wasn't in a position to appreciate that at the time.

Serious health problems continued in the 1990s when I was in my early sixties. Just after we returned from China in late 1991, Lydia noticed a crusty-looking spot on my back. When this was investigated, I was diagnosed with melanoma. This was to be one of three times that I received calls from doctors telling me that I had cancer. In 1992, I had an operation to remove the melanoma. I was told that it was thick and deep in size. It was right in the middle of my back, the result of one too many bad sunburns when I was a boy. After an operation, the area was said to be "clear around the margins" by the doctors at the Surgical Oncology Department of Duke University Hospital. I was under the care of Hilliard Siegler. Dr. Siegler and the Duke program in melanoma treatment had been recommended to me both by my son-in-law, Steven Poplack of the Dartmouth-Hitchcock Medical Center in Hanover, and my dermatologist, John Shrum. Afterward, I agreed to have what was then an experimental treatment for this condition, called specific active immuno therapy. It consisted of four shots into the upper arm, in which I was injected with a substance containing dead melanoma cells designed to reduce the probability of reoccurrence of the melanoma to 50 percent.

I have lived as a cancer patient and survivor ever since. In December 1997, I was diagnosed with prostate cancer, having two cancerous tumors on the gland. On April 1, 1998, I had another operation for prostate cancer. It was discovered that I had "shotty" lymph nodes, perhaps indicating lymphatic cancer. The doctors gave three options for my treatment. During that operation, they decided that I would be sewn up and treated with radiation, instead of having a radical prostatectomy. The doctors hoped that radiation would treat both cancers. After five weeks of radiation, I had the implantation of radioactive pellets, or seeds, which continued the radiation indefinitely. The lymphoma was diagnosed as non-Hodgkin's type. The lymphoma was said by the doctors to be indolent—which reminded me of some of my college students! Lydia and I had a chuckle over this quip. After a bone marrow test, it was determined that there were "highly suspicious lympho-sites" in the lymphatic system. I never had any distinct treatment for my lymphoma. What a blessing that was!

So I had three types of cancer all within the same decade. This caused much anguish and fear in me. In living with this fear and all the attendant anxieties, I was becoming personally developed in a way yet unknown to me. I recall taking long showers and thinking that I needed to prepare to die. How does one make such preparations? That was a big question in my heart. The reality was one of radical psychological insecurity. It was also a spiritual threat to me—my fear of dying. Living with such a state can bring a sense of courage and strength of character.

Late in the 1990s, I developed heart problems, specifically the condition of atrial fibrillation. For a period of six years, this condition was stabilized by the use of a drug known as amiodarone. After the six-year period, for some reason—which was puzzling to my doctors—this drug no longer worked. There then came a long period of energy-sapping tiredness that made my life difficult and unpleasant. We tried every way known to the medical team at the University of Virginia Medical Center's Department of Cardiology.

In the late 1990s, it was discovered that I had an arterial blockage in the lateral descending artery (LDA) of 95 percent. Two stents were put into my heart, which has held up for years. This was not a complicated procedure, nor was it life threatening.

More problematic for me was my condition of A-Fib, which I very much wanted to get out of. I was cardioverted more than once, meaning that I got a mild electric shock to the chest. Later, I was given an ablation procedure through the groin—all to no avail. I was in persistent and stubborn energy-sapping A-Fib. I hated this, and I wanted to do anything possible to rid myself of it. Finally in January 2011, I signed up for the one method that had not been tried—surgical ablation. In this operation, the surgeon would go into my heart through my ribs. He said it would hurt some afterward. I had become suspicious of statements like that from my doctors. Happily, however, I never had to experience that kind of pain, at least that time around.

The day before the procedure, in yet another heart scan, it was discovered that I had another calcium blockage of sixty-five, this in the left main artery. A hybrid operation was performed with a double by-pass procedure, called "rabbit" plus ablation work, both that same day and again two days later, while I was still in the hospital. The doctors referred to this procedure on the blockage as a "widow-maker"!

Soon thereafter, it was discovered that there was a blockage in the vein that had been taken out of my leg and placed in my heart. In another procedure, a stent was inserted in that vein. Soon after that, I found myself to be weak and unsteady on my feet. One night, I fell while getting up from bed and heading for the bathroom. After I hit the floor, I asked my wife if I had fallen. It was discovered that my heart rate was thirty-six, dangerously low. Soon after this, I received a pacemaker.

After some time, when all this had settled down, it was determined that I had graduated from A-Fib to A-Flutter, and after that I entered where I longed to be, in "normal sinus rhythm." I hurled a hurray into the atmosphere and found myself feeling better, with more stability and more energy. I had been in a tiring state of A-Fib for a long time, and I was so relieved.

Back in 2007 in my early seventies, I had another type of medical problem, a subdural hematoma. After treatment for this condition, my left leg was left in a weakened condition. This has contributed to my having some falls, which has bothered me considerably, but which I have managed.

To explain this, I need to go back in time to when we went on a trip to Italy with one of our granddaughters, Emma. I developed a weakness and tiredness. I felt this when our tour included climbing the last mile and a half of Mt. Vesuvius overlooking Pompeii. Trouble was brewing big-time as we descended into Kennedy Airport on our way home. I became disoriented and confused to say the least. We went to our motel in Jamaica Plains, New York, where I lost consciousness and was entirely out of it, with Lydia not being able to stir me. At 3:00 a.m., Lydia called Emma's father, Steven Poplack, a doctor in the Dartmouth-Hitchcock Medical Center in Hanover, New Hampshire, and our daughter Laura's husband. Lydia thought that she might take me into New York City for a stay in a major hospital. Steven advised Lydia to go to somewhere local and very quickly. We went right away to the Jamaica Plains Hospital, where they had a trauma center, and I became an emergency patient.

It was discovered that I had bleeding on the brain. That day I had an emergency operation. It was a life-threatening situation. After returning home, I was under the care of brain specialists who oversaw the process of the excess blood on the brain gradually becoming absorbed. Then I was under the care of a neurologist, concerning problems in my left leg that likely emanated from the hematoma on the right side of my brain. To this day, my left leg is weaker and less in control. During the time from all this to the present, I have fallen several times, mostly tripping and mostly connected with the problems in my left leg.

I live with the fact that I have almost died three times in three different hospitals: the University Memorial Hospital in Chapel Hill, North Carolina, in 1969; the Jamaica Plains Hospital in 2007; and the University of Virginia Medical Center in January 2011. Such a realization has shocked my consciousness and made me think and pray and suffer. Happily now, I live still and better and with more hope and serenity, as my process of becoming has issued into my being in my midseventies.

I believe that things happen for a reason, and that in my becoming, I have developed a more stable health. I believe deep down that this stability came to me for a purpose. To fulfill that purpose, I would enter into and endure the most difficult time—psychologically and spiritually—in my entire life.

Chapter 17: Becoming in My Descent into Darkness

Anger

For most of my life after high school, there has been some level of anger in me—anger at both Dad and Mother. In their lives, particularly after *The Power of Positive Thinking* was published in 1952, they were fundamentally concerned with their most important work, their own reputations, their own influence. Granted they had great work to do; in no way do I wish to downplay that. I fully agree that my dad's work was important. Dad and Mother helped so very many people with their personal problems. And I am proud of them for that. I have been and am proud of how Dad produced highly influential writings and speeches that clearly were so beneficial to so many people. Mother protected him and helped structure organizations that provided channels for the dissemination of his work.

My sisters and I were just children and young people trying to find our own ways. Later after high school, the shocking realization came to me that what I was doing in my life and career had little meaning or value for my parents. I found it demeaning and devaluing to be so regarded by my own parents, whom I loved.

On some level, I came to believe that I wasn't worth much of anything, at least in their eyes. I even came to believe that *I wasn't worth anything* in my own eyes. This was a big problem. Think what that means to feel this way for an independent-minded young person trying to make his own way. After fame set in for my parents, they did not expend energy helping me nourish my own life and work. When we were young and before Dad got famous, we three children had a happy family life with our parents, as I have tried to show.

All of this is the background for something that happened in me that produced my deep anger. At a certain point in time, as I have said before, *I lost something that was terribly important to me*—a close personal relation and connection with my dad. I never got it back. It was supremely frustrating that this happened, and there seemed to be nothing I could do about it. Decisions that I made, which I felt were good for me, were apparently regarded by my parents, especially by Dad, as bad decisions and somehow difficult for them to understand and accept. For example, there was my decision to go to Union Theological Seminary in New York. I chose to go to an educational institution that they felt was bad for them. Witness the letter that my father wrote to me at that time. He could not understand what I was doing. All he saw about me was that I was going "into the seat of his most implacable enemies." He was thinking only of himself at this most difficult time in his life. That is understandable. He did, however, end that letter so filled with pathos, "Love, Dad." Then he personally backed off away from me, and Mother backed off with him. I was left on my own with little or no parental approval, encouragement, or involvement in regard to my career for much of the rest of my life.

Finding my way in life under these conditions became a most important, difficult, and frustrating endeavor. But find my way, I did, and that has seemed so right and good for me. Yet I have had to live with the reality that the role my parents played in all of this was largely negative. Because of this, I had to live with a frustration and a lack of a sense of personal value that I found hard to understand. And if I ever wrote a letter to Dad telling him what I could not understand, I would sign it, "Love, John."

It may be said or thought that I have overstated this matter. Perhaps this may be so for others. I don't know about what others think; that is none of my own business. I am talking about my sense of my own life. *My feelings became depressed, my spirits became dissolute, and my life went down into darkness, despair, and then into active alcoholism.* Those have been the dark realities for me. When I hit my bottom in alcoholism, I was desperate and could see no way out. This desperation was horrible, as I will soon describe. I have been in the process of recovery for over twelve years since then, and life is better to be sure. One fact remains:

never again do I want to be the way I was at my bottom in the early spring of 2000. I never want to feel that way again or to be in that kind of situation. I have now found a good life in which I am recovering from that emphatically terrible state.

I go back in my feelings to remember how it was when I was a boy, living with my sisters and parents in our apartment at Forty-Fifth Avenue in New York City. As I have shown, I have good memories of that time and the family's times in Pawling, New York, in our Quaker Hill home. This was before my high school years, when things were largely happy.

It was, however, the time when I discovered the harsh reality that it seemed like the only thing having any worth in our family was what Dad was doing! Later in life, I found a deep level of anger over the fact that Dad hardly ever gave me any encouragement or support in my career. Of course, we all live concurrently on many levels at once. I was succeeding in my career, with much satisfaction and pride for that. At the same time, I found myself in an anxious, worrisome state over the loss of contact with and support from my dad.

With our own children, Lydia and I have tried to act differently. We actively sought to find out what our children wanted to do in life and to talk to them about their lives in this way. When we were confident that they were sincere in their desires, we were unfailingly supportive, particularly for good work of use to society, we were solidly behind them all the way. We sought ways to aid them in their pursuits, and that has gone on the whole of their lives. I never felt such support from my parents. I have asked myself many times whether there was some basic element of parenting that my parents failed so badly. True, they were doing work that was deeply helpful to so many. Yet I was seemingly shunted aside and left on my own. I missed the personal contact with my dad that I once had. I became deeply frustrated and angry. Since there was absolutely nothing I could do about this situation, I became depressed. Life became dark and desperate.

In all of this, I came to feel I was being held back in developing my own career goals. These constant and nagging states in me kept me from fully developing my talents and my life. And there were the persistent questions. Why had I chosen a field so difficult for my father, and why couldn't I rise above that problem in my own work? I kept feeling that Dad was holding me back from a higher level of academic development. This all happened just as I was being frustrated and separated from him, when what I wanted was to be close to him. I couldn't understand why I couldn't go off in my own way and yet be loved and accepted by my dad, even though it was not "following in my father's footsteps." This added to my anger and frustration on a deep level through much of my adult and professional life.

The Onset of Alcoholism

My parents once told us three children that they would give us $2,000 each if we did not drink or smoke until we were twenty-one years of age. None of us ever collected that money! My first drinks were in my high school years. In my late twenties, I started drinking alcohol in a different way than ever before. This came after theological seminary in 1963 when Lydia and I established a home in Chicago. As I have shown, this was a time of personal and professional uncertainty and indecision. I started drinking more heavily. It all started with the proverbial "couple of drinks" before dinner and then with wine with dinner. The drinking gradually increased over the years to more drinks before dinner, more wine with dinner, and more after-dinner drinks. Always wanting more is one major hallmark of an alcoholic life.

Lydia and I had a young family in Chicago and were enjoying that—oh, so much fun with two young daughters and one son, all bright-eyed and full of fun. We both enjoyed these years in our condominium unit, which surrounded a courtyard in which the kids could play safely.

And we had a good life in the "Windy City," also named the "Second City" after a noted comedy theatrical show north of the Chicago downtown Loop. We watched the seasons come and go, Chicago style, seemingly hot until one day it turned cold, and then colder, until one day it turned hot. We enjoyed the arts in Chicago, particularly the music at the Symphony Hall on Michigan Avenue and the displays at the Art Institute.

We enjoyed the politics, finding ourselves in anti-Mayor Daley demonstrations. We got involved in race relations, in those heady days in the 1960s when "Operation Bread Basket" was in full swing. Dr. Martin Luther King came to town, saying that Chicago was a suburb of Mississippi.

We especially enjoyed the community of Hyde Park in the city, an interesting and diverse place. It was a "Negro suburb." It was there that Dick Gregory lived. It was he, with some irony, who declared that Hyde

Park was a place where blacks and whites stood arm-in-arm against the poor.

I enjoyed courses that I took at the University of Chicago, stimulating the academic and scholarly side of my personality. I have previously described some of the highly influential courses I took at that famous academic institution, all given by people of academic and personal stature. Lydia enjoyed her teaching job at the North Shore Country Day School. We both found a worshipping community in Hyde Park, the Hyde Park Methodist Church, with our friend Rev. Joe Buckles as minister. It was he whom I invited to preach my ordination service at the Marble Collegiate Church in 1965, in which my dad gave the charge to me as a candidate for ordination.

As I have described, I enjoyed my job at Elmhurst College just west of the city. I had this job from 1965 to 1968. It was there that I fell off that fence to the side of academics and teaching. I discovered that I loved teaching and was good at it and fulfilled by it. I conceived it as a form of ministry in academia, in which I could be myself and do good work that was helpful to many. In my classes and in my more personal relationship with students, I found meaning and purpose. I got a sense of my own value and meaning. It was at Elmhurst that I became a good teacher, and I looked forward to a satisfying career in this field of teaching philosophy.

But all this time, my drinking was on the increase with frequency of nights that I was out of it and under the influence of alcohol. Many nights at home, I was getting high or drunk. I do not mean to suggest that I was taking drugs. Drug addiction has not and is not my problem. My substance of choice has been alcohol all along. There were an increasing number of times that I just disappeared and went upstairs and went to sleep early, before or when I was passing out. I don't remember, however, many times when my drinking was a disturbingly negative matter with the family. The awareness of this came to me quite strongly at a later time. I was living my way into alcoholic habits.

We moved from Chicago to Chapel Hill, North Carolina, in 1968, and the same pattern continued. I don't think that I had yet crossed the line into alcoholism even during this period. It is difficult for this alcoholic to look back and to determine when that oh-so-important line was crossed. One of the key indicators whether that line has been crossed is that point at which one loses the power of choice in drinking. I lost that power of choice. In Chicago and Chapel Hill, as I look back, there was still time for me to stop drinking or at least to retard or prevent the onset of alcoholism.

I believe that it was during the 1970s at some point that I crossed over the line and became an alcoholic and also became even more of a deeply angry and depressed man. I recall years later going to a twelve-step meeting when I was just newly sober in Charlottesville, and I was boiling over with anger. In response to a suggestion by the leader for any "burning desires" to open the meeting, I poured out my anger, openly weeping in the process. The response was revealing, as many other alcoholics in that meeting showed and told about their own anger in a huge rush of emotion, which dominated the whole meeting.

So I was angry, what's new? Alcoholics typically have deep anger. It's difficult to explain to a nonalcoholic what a real alcoholic is so angry about. It is a complicated matter. It can be said that I was angry because I didn't fit in with so much in life, and I so deeply resented my dad and mother for the specific reasons I have mentioned—plus so many more factors beneath the level of consciousness.

It may appear that in the earlier part of this book, I show that I fit quite well into life, in that I had a loving family and was a runner and active in politics and other engagements. As an alcoholic, it is clear to me that I did not fit in with life, in the sense that even given all of this, I was not comfortable in my own skin. I was filled with worries and anxieties, many associated with my long effort to find my way apart from my dad. I felt that I needed the release and the escape that alcohol gave me, or seemed to give me for a while.

In 1971, we moved to Virginia, and we have never left this beautiful state. It was here that I got a job at Stratford College while I was finishing my PhD at the University of North Carolina. During these three years, until 1974, we lived in Danville, Virginia. Stratford closed in 1974. Happily, Lydia got a job teaching English at Chatham Hall, a boarding school for girls in Chatham, Virginia, some twenty miles north of Danville.

During the time in Virginia, I was drinking more and more heavily. For the first time, I believe, I was having personal problems with my wife and children due to my drinking. I felt supremely frustrated at the condition that was developing in me. Now I knew what was happening to me, but then *I was powerless to stop drinking* and to change my ways. And the anger that developed toward my dad began playing back upon itself, becoming itself a mushrooming general emotional state. I passed through specific anger at my dad. My anger became a central personal condition; it became the real me. All the attendant problems—including my sense of being devalued, of feeling that I wasn't worth anything, of being so deeply frustrated—powerfully disturbed me. And I was supremely frustrated at what my drinking was doing to me and my family and angry also about my utter inability to let liquor alone. These feelings and states in me existed apart from and in addition to my resentments at my parents.

All this became dominant in my life. Why couldn't I stop drinking? Why did I have to be so angry? The anger was like a cancer within me, eating away at me from the insides. I began to obsess about and over it, getting more and more deeply depressed in the process. I had crossed the line into alcoholism. It is an amazing thing for me or for any alcoholic—that I got depressed as I was pouring so much of the depressant drug into my system!

In 1976, due to job difficulties and my more deeply personal problems, I became suicidal. That year, I was commuting from Chatham, where our family lived on the campus of Chatham Hall westward to Ferrum. My job that year was at Ferrum College in Virginia, a small college where I got a job after Stratford closed. This was not a satisfying job; it was something I considered a stopgap until I could get another good job on a tenure track at a place I really considered suitable for me.

The road from Chatham to Ferrum was along Route 29, turning west on Route 40, headed toward Ferrum in the mountains of western Virginia, indeed a lovely setting. Route 40 heading west from Gretna had roller-coaster hills aplenty. It was mostly when I was returning home that I had the suicidal thoughts. As I sped down hills or came up the same, I faced tractor-trailer trucks coming at me. The problem for me was whether or not I could get past these trucks. I had to avoid the strong suicidal impulse of running into them and ending the pain. I was in cold sweats and shivering and feeling like I was going down. I felt scared. I don't know how I did it, but I did get by those trucks. Here I am to tell about it.

My drinking continued and increased, and the anger became mixed with a deepening depression. I had gone way beyond just being angry at Dad. I remember bad times for me and the family, when I would sit in our living room listening to music, perhaps Duke Ellington or the Modern Jazz Quartet. I was thinking deeply. This was the drunken state of a philosopher. I thought of the logic of Aristotle, who had a principle of the excluded middle. I could sense the excluded middle between contradictory propositions collapsing into each other in a Hegelian-type synthesis between thesis and antithesis. Obviously, during these times, I was oblivious to the needs and interests of my family. *I was in a world alone, all about me—selfish and self-centered to the extreme.*

There is an irony here that in becoming so self-absorbed, selfish, and self-centered, I was becoming like Dad, who was so full of himself in his life as a famous and influential person. I exhibited alcoholic behavior in blowing off steam in anger, or in sulking when I didn't get my way. Ironically, this sort of behavior was like that of my dad. In my troubled alcoholic state, I could not give the kind of support to my wife and kids that they deserved. Dad couldn't do this either. My whole alcoholic life was, however, independent of my dad and mother. I was different in my alcoholism from Dad, yet similar in my behavior to his ways of acting. I wondered if they ever knew about my alcoholism, but I have no evidence that they did. My family, especially Lydia and our three children, suffered from it. My sisters knew about it, to be sure, and also were hurt from it.

For the first time, I took my problems into the office of a psychiatrist at the Memorial Hospital in Chapel Hill, named Dr. Hunter. How was I going to get out of the depressing cycle I was in? I was drinking late in the afternoon, through dinner and the evening, under the influence of alcohol most of the evening, going to sleep or passing out, waking up the next morning, feeling awful and promising myself that I wouldn't do that the next day. During those days, everything I did was designed to make myself feel better, and when noon rolled around, after lunch with some exercise I did feel better, but then I started the drinking again, and again the cycle continued. It lasted for years.

I was hurting my family, especially my children. I recall in the early to mideighties when I was teaching at Longwood College, how I came home after class and started to drink. Our middle school or high school children came home from school to find Dad under the influence or drunk at home, usually sitting in the living room with my sound system going strong with music, such as "Blues on Bach," with me engaging in what I would call "deep thinking," but what was really a drunken stupor.

What were the kids to do? I now realize that most days they didn't bring their friends home. They usually scattered to their rooms. The creativity and fun of the family was being sucked out of the house and damaged as Dad was drinking. Oh, how I have been guilty and ashamed about this for years! I only got beyond that guilt and shame years later, working the steps of a twelve-step program with another alcoholic who had committed to helping me.

Then in 1997, as I have described in a preceding section, I was diagnosed with two types of cancer, prostate and lymphoma, for which I received treatment during the last three years of the 1990s. Previously, in 1992, I had had a thick and deep melanoma, which had been treated and was not showing any external signs.

So into the mix of anger and depression was added another strong and confusing negative emotion into my consciousness—fear related to my precarious health situation. I remember taking long showers and feeling scared that I was going to die.

We went to a cancer center appointment at the University of Virginia with a conference of doctors. In the examining room, my blood pressure was taken, and it was near stroke levels.

Lydia and I walked out of that appointment dazed and scared, not knowing what to do. We went shopping, and she bought an expensive lovely linen jacket, turquoise to go with her blue eyes. I picked out a fine set of dress chopsticks in an impressive display. Then we went out to an expensive dinner at a fancy restaurant, enjoying the fine dining and subtle tastes and textures of well-prepared dinner dishes. This type of activity gave us some immediate but temporary relief.

It was in these circumstances that Lydia and I traveled to New York City, to the Marble Collegiate Church, for a service commemorating the one hundredth year since Dad's birth. I had passed into a low state of anger and depression, passing beyond the specific anger I had toward my father and mother in my earlier years. That, however, made it even more difficult for me to deal with what I was to confront on this occasion in New York.

Interlude 3:
Suffering at an Important
Anniversary of My Dad

O n this occasion, celebrating the one-hundredth anniversary of
Dad's birth, that is May 31, 1998, I did not give a speech. It was a
service of worship, with a focus on praise and adulation of my dad, his
life, and career. The whole family was gathered at Marble Church where
we grew up. It was a public event with a full congregation of more than
twelve hundred people. It was also a family event for a large number
of people, including many of our children, my two sisters, and some
grandkids as well. It was a time of happiness, celebration, and many
good important memories for the family.

In the pastor's pew, I sat with Lydia and other members of the
family, including Mother. I was blown away emotionally as we heard the
praise and saw videos of Dad's preaching. These video clips went back
into time, when he was younger and really powerful in his preaching.
They came from the time when I was a boy, sitting in the same pew,
looking up at my father with pride and love.

But this time I could feel a cringe in my gut, with all that anger and
depression I was currently experiencing, together with my heavy, out-of-
control drinking. I was transfixed in emotional pain. I sat upright in rapt
concentration on the images of Dad preaching with full gesticulations
and modulation of his voice. As usual, he talked with an appealing

self-deprecating humor, gaining thereby a personal connection with the people in his view.

After the service, the family retired into a private drawing room off a hallway behind the pulpit end of the sanctuary. This was a time of a break for the family before a public reception. I sat stretched out on a couch with my head back, emotionally hurting. I don't know what I looked like at that moment. I do remember vividly that a kind woman from the Marble Collegiate Church staff came up to me and asked if I needed medical attention. I was surprised and quickly declined the offer. I forced myself to sit up straight and look more attentive. The family was having a good time all around me, but I wasn't a part of that.

All the years of trying to find my own way in life, of trying to recapture a closeness with my dad, all the bad experiences—all the anger and depression and darkness was beginning to come to haunt me in a big way. At this occasion at Marble, where I felt so at home as a boy, I was in a dangerous and desperate place. I felt that I simply had to endure my time there and get away with as little notice and attention as possible. I felt like I needed to get away from the home base of my dad and mother and family background. I looked forward very much to returning to Virginia, where I felt that I was somebody, even in my depressed condition. Perhaps I could figure out what was happening to me in the present state of my alcoholism and in my sense of desperation at this important anniversary of my dad's at Marble.

With the assistance of my psychiatrist in Charlottesville, named Abraham, and his astute analysis of my psychological and spiritual condition, I came to realize that *what I was feeling at the time was shame.* My father was so powerful in his talented presentation; I felt that I was a big fat nothing, sinking down as I was into a quagmire of alcoholic despair. I had suffered with anger over our loss of contact. I had become depressed, for I saw no way out of this predicament. I couldn't see how to get out of my seemingly hopeless state of body and mind into which my alcoholism had led me. I was alone, separated and withdrawn in the company of my very own family whom I loved and who loved me.

Somehow I got through that occasion, but I didn't know what the family thought of me—if anything. I guessed that all I needed to do was to survive and leave after the service, which I did with entirely negative and emotionally desperate feelings.

Chapter 18: Becoming in Despair and Alcoholism

We alcoholics usually tell our stories following a three-part outline suggested in a twelve-step program: "what we used to be like, what happened, and what we are like now." The "what we used to be like" usually takes a form we call a "drunkalog."

I had my first drink in the summer of 1951, after my freshman year at Deerfield. I had invited a Deerfield friend, Bayard Halsted, to our family home on Quaker Hill. One night, we went out and "had a few beers." I don't remember how many beers I actually drank. I do recall reeling and weaving all over the country road coming back from our escapade and walking toward our home, clearly under the influence. I was feeling that "buzz." I also was composing a speech I would say to Dad should I meet him. Happily, I did not meet him. Instead, Bayard and I went to a room over our garage where there were pool and ping-pong tables. My sister Maggie happened to come up to play, and sensing the situation with me, quickly disappeared.

My drinking continued as I have indicated in my section on early married life. At this point, we alcoholics give our "drunkalog," laying out in detail our drinking history with all the crazy things we did and the bad choices we made. Instead of this usual procedure, what I would like to recall is the several times I got into public trouble due to my drinking.

In the summer of 1971, our family was vacationing at the Outer Banks of North Carolina. We had rented two houses, and both my sisters and their families were there. I was engaging in a time-tested alcoholic activity there, that is, crossing the bridge from the mainland to the Outer Banks for vacation and then drinking. Generally, we had a wonderful time together, except for the land breeze that brought the bugs in abundance.

One night after a Colonel Sanders fried-chicken dinner on our deck, my brother-in-law, John Allen, and I went out to get a needed bottle of milk. I was driving, and we stopped in a convenience store to buy the milk. Due to my condition, perhaps, I did not notice the patrolman in the store, nor did I notice that he followed us after we left. Apparently, I was weaving all over the road, and the next thing I remember is the blue lights flashing behind me. We were stopped, and I was ticketed, taken to the police station, and given a court date. I can't now remember what I blew on the machine the police use to determine the level of alcohol in the bloodstream.

All of this resulted in the charge of a DUI, a serious charge indeed. A court date was set for early fall. I lived with the problem, and drank over it, but did largely stay off the road when drinking. It was embarrassing to go to the court with my hired lawyer and have him describe what a good character I had, and then listen to the judge openly wondering with biting sarcasm how a person of such good character could end up as I had. Fortunately, at that point, I did not have any evidence of drunk driving on my record. The upshot of the trial was that with the help of my lawyer, the charge was reduced to reckless driving. It was also embarrassing when I told my employer at Stratford College of the whole incident. At least I was honest.

During the next decade, I was an everyday drinker, or so my family pointed out. There was a pattern during the eighties, when we were living in Farmville, where I was doing my job, where I was drinking regularly, and where I even was becoming a "distinguished" professor of philosophy at Longwood College. This daily pattern produced a guilt in me that lasted for years.

During these years, I was seeing a psychiatrist in Richmond once a week. After a while, it became clear that this counseling, although quite helpful to me generally, was not having the effect on me that my family desired. The counselor's technique seemed designed to help me to drink responsibly. He expressed pride in his record of controlling the drinking problems of his patients. My family did not like the situation. One day at lunch in a public restaurant, they intervened and confronted me with the problem of drinking and the lack of good effect of my counseling. They insisted that I stop seeing this particular psychiatrist.

Another big incident happened in the mid-1990s when I was in my college office in the evening, drinking after a frustrating call with my parents and sisters. Our mother was taking control of our finances in a way that was frustrating to me and which caused such deep resentments. I hung up very angry and went out to get another bottle of gin to further fortify myself. Soon I decided that I wanted to go to Chapel Hill, where I had graduated with my PhD degree. For reasons that escape me, or for no reason at all, I drove south, heading toward Chapel Hill. In my confusion and alcoholic soaked brain, I believed that there was a philosophy meeting there, which I thought I would attend. I didn't realize that there were no philosophy meetings in the middle of the night!

Just a few miles away, I pulled off the main road onto a smaller road and headed toward Hampden Sydney College, where I went into a ditch on the left side of the road and passed out. Neither I nor the car received any physical damage. I was rudely awakened by a bright flashlight shining in the window, focusing on my face and the nearly empty pint bottle of gin on the passenger's seat next to me. Blue lights were flashing all around. I was arrested and taken to the police station in nearby Farmville.

I recall a couple of things—first, that the couple whose ditch I slightly damaged came and recognized me as the son of Norman Vincent Peale. They were reported to have said something like this: "My God, what is this world coming to?" Then Charles Scott, dean of students at Hampden Sydney College, was called by a friendly Hampden-Sydney college policeman. On his own initiative, he came to the police station, and I was released into his custody. I, a "distinguished" Longwood College professor, came this close to spending a night in the Farmville jail!

My lawyer from Farmville took me through the case when I was officially charged with a DUI. No reduction of the penalty this time around. One telling point is that I remember his saying that he thought he would probably see me again in a similar incident. By court order, I was enrolled in a state of Virginia "Alcoholic Safety Action Program" or ASAP, for my first of three treatment programs.

In the late 1990s, perhaps around the time of attending the celebration of the one-hundredth anniversary of Dad's birth at Marble

Church, I had another drinking and driving incident. Lydia and I attended a sophisticated party at the Boar's Head Club in Charlottesville, sponsored by the Virginia Foundation of the Humanities, where Lydia served on the board. Graciously, before dinner, I offered to get Lydia a glass of wine, and during that absence from her, I quickly drank some glasses of wine. I refilled Lydia's glass once more, as I downed another couple glasses of wine. Then we had a good dinner, replete with interesting conversation and with no more alcohol for me.

During this time, I was on the drug Ativan, prescribed by my Richmond psychiatrist for anxiety. The combination of this substance and the wine I had consumed proved dangerous. On the way home when I was driving, I was weaving all over the road. Lydia was scared, and she kept telling me to slow down and to stop weaving. Apparently someone called the police about our car, and as we were turning to the gate of Lake Monticello, I was stopped again by the police.

As it turned out, he cut me some slack. He said he could smell nothing on my breath, and he gave me a warning. If I had received another DUI, it would have meant the loss of my driver's license. This was fortunate for me, or so I thought at the time. It was fortunate at least in the short run. Perhaps the greater punishment would have awakened me to my honest problem. Perhaps I could have realized then that I really did need to stop drinking. But that good decision was put off. I was not desperate enough yet.

During this time, I voluntarily entered an out-patient alcohol treatment program at "First Step" on Pantops Mountain in Charlottesville. We met four times a week at 5:00 p.m., with Wednesdays off. I "passed" this program, seemingly with flying colors; at least that was the perception of some of the staff. Secretly, I had been drinking some in the evenings after many of these sessions. I was careful not to drink much, so I would not register alcohol on my breath when I blew in the machine at the beginning of each session.

One night at home with Lydia was particularly bad. I found myself passed out cold on the tile floor off our kitchen, with bruises on my sides and shoulders. I cannot remember how I got there or how I got my bruises. I do recall that I was dressed only in a pair of undershorts. Most importantly, I remember Lydia rousing me into consciousness and looking down at me with fire in her eyes. She was angry, hurt, and worried sick. By my actions over time, I had brought her to this state. On this occasion, I recall her talking to Laura about me and how bad things were. I will never forget how she looked as she held out the telephone, demanding that I explain myself to my oldest daughter. She wanted me to do something, but I didn't want to talk to anyone in that condition. I just wanted to lie on that cold tile floor and have her go away and leave me alone, let me stew in my radical loneliness in my drunken state. But she was too angry to let me off. Her eyes were hard and wildly energized with hurt and anger. I don't recall how the incident ended, but it was not positive. Somehow we went on together.

Another incident occurred during Thanksgiving vacation of 1999, when Lydia and I were in Georgia with Lydia's sister Ann. One day, while away from the home supposedly to work on an academic paper, I started drinking wine after lunch, and then I drank throughout the afternoon. We had the usual predinner hard drinks and then wine with dinner. After that, I decided that I was going to drive to a twelve-step program meeting about a mile away. On the way, I bought another pint of gin and drank some of that.

I never got to the meeting; I "fell sleep" in the car at the meeting site. When I woke a couple of hours later, I managed, I know not how, to drive home and to park the car in the driveway. I then passed out. Lydia, who was worried and still up, came out to get me. She could not budge me from the car. I was not cooperative. I was thinking only of myself. All I wanted was to rest. There was hell to pay in the morning. I seriously promised Lydia that if I relapsed again I would accept being sent to a residential treatment center.

That final relapse came on March 9, 2000, when Lydia came home from an evening out, only to find a fresh cork from a newly opened bottle of wine on the rug at our front door. While she was away, I had drunk more after our dinner and had again thought of going to a twelve-step program meeting. I again passed out before the meeting at the site. I was torn apart, wanting to drink more, always more, and yet to go to my twelve-step meetings to do something about my drinking. But I fell asleep in the car. After some time, I was able to drive home.

I "hit my bottom" on that same night of March 9, 2000, at the site of that meeting in Palmyra. All the anger that had built up over the years—not only about my parents, but about many other things, including the super frustration of not having been able to do anything on my own about my drinking—brought me down. I had become deeply depressed. The combination of the anger and depression had become very dangerous.

All through this time, I was deluded, thinking that I could stop drinking if I really wanted to, and my problems and resentments could be eased—resolved. I did not realize the level of denial of my basic condition. I kept thinking that I could lick this drink thing, that I was *not* powerless over alcohol after all. I kept thinking that all the way down to my desperation of spirit. Now I understand that I had to get really desperate to break the denial. I did not see that I could never get my resentments eased and resolved until I stopped drinking and began to work on those sorts of feelings. Everything was seen as an excuse to drink more, so how could I ever do without alcohol in my life?

The anger and depression produced in me a darkness of soul. I felt that my life was going down. I was going down, and there wasn't any way that I could think of to do anything about the problem. I was scared, for I didn't know what was to become of me. In a sense, I was dying. I was desperate, for I didn't know what to do to get me out of this horrible psychological and spiritual state. Life was dark. Emotionally, I was descending into darkness with no support, nothing solid on which to be grounded. I was in Nothingness, Darkness, and Despair.

There is an old joke that didn't apply to me. It is a story about a guy who tripped in the woods and fell headlong down into a deep dark pit. On the way down, he was able to grab onto a piece of the root of a tree protruding from the sides of the pit. He held onto it for dear life. After some thought, he called up, asking if there was anybody up there who could help him. Finally a voice came loud and clear: I am the God of Abraham, Isaac, and Jacob. I can help you. If you but let go and fall, I will lift you up. The man thought a bit and then said, "Is there anyone else up there?"

For me, there was nothing to catch and hold on to. I was falling and going down. I was desperate in feelings I never ever want to feel again. Then a good, yet frightening, realization came to me. I really was powerless. On that terrible occasion, something good happened to me; I felt powerlessness to the root of my being. I haven't had a drink since that night, as of this writing more than twelve years later.

Chapter 19: Becoming in Recovery and Counseling

One or two days later, I attended a morning twelve-step program meeting in Charlottesville. During the meeting, I found myself "sharing" and openly weeping at the same time. I found myself saying that my life had come to a big fat nothing, and I was scared. I told about my life and about how I felt. One perceptive "old timer," named Phil, came to me after the meeting, put his hands on my shoulders, and shook me hard, getting my attention. He said something tough but what later proved to be wonderful. He said: *"John, you will never get anywhere until you get beyond the guilt and the shame."* I realized that feeling demeaned and worthless, and guilty for what I had done in my drinking life, and ashamed for what I was in that life—all this was bringing me down. How was I ever going to "get beyond" all of this? In my recovery, I have, by the grace of God, realized that I am not demeaned or nothing. The good news is that I really have "gotten beyond" the shame and the guilt.

The next day, Lydia and I met with a counselor from Pantops named Al Wood. I was ready to fulfill my promise to Lydia—that if I relapsed again, I would get help. Reluctantly, and with considerable hesitation, I agreed to go into a residential treatment center. I was scared about what all this meant and anxious about what the treatment center would be like. Also, I had the strong sense that I owed Lydia this effort to do something about my drinking, and I wanted the children to be aware of the constructive effort I was making to change things for the better.

Al made the arrangements for me, on March 15, 2000, to enter Williamsburg Place in Williamsburg, Virginia, initially for a period of one month. After I was there for a short while, this got extended to a three-month stay of intensive alcoholic treatment work. It was said that I was a "chronic relapser" and that I was "a hard case." When I first entered Williamsburg Place, I was scared, still not knowing what was going to happen to me. I did, however, sense that I was finally doing something good about my drinking.

I did not like it very much in the treatment center. Yet I realized soon enough that it might give me a good foundation for sobriety. There was an artificial environment in the treatment center to be sure, with a diverse group of people, mostly of the professional type. The program was challenging, demanding, difficult. But ultimately, I saw that it was good for me. My case manager, named James, did his best to help me and the others get in touch with our feelings, to stop the persistent denial, and to become more honest with ourselves. We had daily small-group sessions, large meetings with the staff, and a variety of activities, which lasted from 8:00 a.m. to midevening every day.

We shared together and cried together, worried and began to feel some progress together. At times, we were threatened and challenged— and other times inspired. We both laughed and cried together. The group dynamics were challenging to be sure. One thing I found out was that each of us was thinking primarily about ourselves, in our selfish, self-centered states. It set up clashes between strong personalities that surfaced regularly. I found that I was older than most and suffered from some displaced resentments that some of the men had with their fathers. Of course, I could absolutely identify with that due to the resentment I had toward my dad. This helped me to accept, even to share, their resentments.

One especially difficult time was on "family day" when our three children came to the center for a day of confrontation. Lydia was upset about some things she found out. Most difficult for me was a session I had with Laura, Clifford, and Lacy—alone with me and James. I was thinking that my presence at this place would impress them, that Dad was finally doing something about his drinking. What I found, especially from Laura, but from each in turn, was an outpouring of resentments against me and my drinking. They told me and James exactly and in threatening detail just how they felt about my drinking behavior toward them and in relation to their own children. I found myself hurt and certainly on the defensive. For me, the session was predominately negative, but James thought it more positive. My children were getting things off their chests. After a while, I said I thought we had better end the session and that the three children ought to leave. As they drove away, I realized what an unhappy moment it was for them as well as for me. James helped me to see the mutual love that came through all the criticism and sensitivity. For years, this has remained a sensitive issue—and a bad memory—between me and Laura, Cliff, and Lacy.

Early in June 2000, I left Williamsburg Place. Lydia and I did something special by going to Charleston, South Carolina, to attend the Spoleto Music Festival held there each year in June. I enjoyed all the young musical talent at the festival, but I also was scared that out again, independent in the world, I might drink again. How could I not drink? It was in Charleston that I started going regularly to twelve-step meetings. I found solid comfort in the sharing by people in these meetings. I made a significant discovery, that many of their stories were just like my own. Most importantly, I glimpsed and had a sense of a Higher Power available in the fellowship for each of us in the twelve-step program. It became a "we" program, working together for the good of members of the group.

When I got back home to Charlottesville, I started to throw myself into the twelve-step program by attending meetings, reading and rereading the literature, and meditating and praying. Not too long after, a man named Amos came to me, suggesting that he could be my sponsor. His honesty and clarity impressed me, and I felt that working with him could be a good thing for me. With him, I began to work the steps, and important things began to happen, ever so slowly at first. I was taking tentative baby-like steps. My new life began, slowly and with great difficulty, to change for the better. Amos is still my sponsor today, and he has also become a good friend. We connect on a deep personal level. Sometimes I feel that we have become transparent with each other—that he can see, as it were, right through me. Sometimes our roles seem to get reversed, as I have shared my experience, strength, and hope with him, as if I were his sponsor. Or we are cosponsoring each other in our honest, caring, and probing discussions together.

When newly sober back home, I found that my feelings were all over the place, up and down and all around. I could see that I was still caught in the state of selfishness and self-centeredness. Most importantly, it seemed that everything I did was designed to make me feel better. I felt that I was walking on eggshells. Life was insecure, anxious, and worrisome. But good day after good day came and went; I was not drinking. As with many other alcoholics in this situation, the feelings that I had dulled so deeply in my drinking days came roaring back, and I felt threatened, being high and elated or alternatively low and down most all the time.

The First Step of the program was this: "We admitted that we were powerless over alcohol—that our lives had become unmanageable." It was a first requirement that I accept my powerlessness in all its forms. In my experience at my bottom, I admitted—and felt to the core of my being—my powerlessness in all its forms. My life had certainly become unmanageable in that I never knew exactly when I was going to drink, and when drinking, I never knew when it was enough. I took step one.

As a son of Norman Vincent Peale and one familiar with his work, I could see that there was a special problem in my taking step one. Twelve-step people working the steps have to learn that self-confidence is of no value in overcoming an alcoholic problem. It would seem that the same can be said of "positive thinking." One does not get sober, nor did I not get sober by thinking positively. I got sober by accepting my powerlessness and by not drinking, one day at a time. This seems like a contradiction between my dad's point of view and the outlook in the twelve-step program. I had to opt for the latter to get sober. After that, positive thinking was a definite help in working the rest of the steps.

As one important reading in a twelve-step program piece of literature has it, it is a lesson in practical humility to take situations in life as they are, myself as I am, and other people as they are. When I was drinking, I could do none of these three things. I found that this acceptance was the answer to all my problems. As a twelve-step program literature says:

> And acceptance is the answer to all my problems today. When I am disturbed, it is because I find some person, place, thing, or situation—some fact of my life—unacceptable to me, and I can find no serenity until I accept that person, place, or thing, or situation as being exactly the way it is supposed to be at this moment. Nothing, absolutely nothing, happens in God's world by mistake. Until I could accept my alcoholism, I could not stay sober; unless I accept

my life completely on life's terms, I cannot be happy. I need
to concentrate not so much on what needs to be changed
in the world as on what needs to be changed in me and in
my attitudes.

Early on in my sobriety, I was advised to read this passage every day. I
followed that advice for many a day.

Such work on the first step wasn't easy—and that is a big
understatement. In the three lessons in practical humility, I found that
accepting other people, especially Dad and Mother, was a most difficult
thing. I still had my deep and obsessive anger, even though I could feel
that my depression was ever so slowly beginning to lift.

The Second Step in the twelve-step program required that I "came to
believe that a Power greater than ourselves could restore us to sanity."
As a religious person, I have had no trouble believing in a Power greater
than me. As people in a twelve-step program say, "God exists, and He is
not I." I have affirmed this all my life. As an alcoholic, I have been insane
in the sense that I have acted as though and believed that I could do the
same things—drink—and not get the same results. I came to see that
I had to stop drinking, and that under those conditions, the insanity
would begin to be eradicated by the belief that God or my Higher Power
can "restore us to sanity."

Ever since 1999, I have been in counseling, seeing a psychiatrist or
psychoanalyst in Charlottesville, named Abraham. We started working
together three times a week, before we moved down to two times and
then to only one time each week. We started together at the height of
my drinking career, when I was vulnerable and down. We have worked
together all the years up to the present time. Being counseled by him
and actively participating in a twelve-step program has coordinated
well together. He is about my age and is from New York, and we are
both avid sports fans, although not of the same teams. He was a fan of
the New York Giants, and I of the Brooklyn Dodgers. He is a fan of the
Virginia Cavaliers basketball program, and I of the North Carolina Tar
Heels. We have connected on a deep and close personal level. We can
openly kid each other. And I am so grateful for his wise and creative
counsel. Reasons for that gratitude will become more evident as my
narrative continues.

Step Three of a twelve-step program states: "Made a decision to turn our will and lives to the care of God as we understood Him." The last phrase is designed to be very important and to open the twelve-step program up to all sorts of views of God or a Higher Power. This has helped keep it inclusive and nonrestrictive. Twelve-step program people do not like to be told what to do or what to believe.

When I came to this step, working with Amos, I found one huge difficulty. I was like the man talked about in another of the writings of a twelve-step program. Reference is made to a person "full of faith but still reeking of alcohol." That was me. The problem was that my faith alone could not seem to overcome my drinking problem. I felt that I had been taking step three most all my life, in my sincere attempt to turn my life and my problems over to God in Jesus Christ. So I felt that at that time, and under those circumstances, I could not take step three. My sponsor, Amos, suggested a solution. Perhaps, he said, I could take step three by going on and taking steps four and five and six. That worked for me.

The Fourth Step says: "Made a searching and fearless moral inventory of ourselves." I had to confront my anger and depression, mostly the former. According to a twelve-step program literature, there is the method of the three columns and two other passages that we use for this process. In this complete process, I see that there are five points in the literature: who I am resentful or angry at, what is the cause of this anger, how does it affect me, what is my part in this resentment, and what can I do about it to make things better. Perhaps it is already clear some of what needs to be said about some of these factors in step four.

What I needed to do was to work through, to understand, and to get a sense of the anger I felt. As I have said, it was an internal affair, an anger that ate away at me from the inside. I obsessed over it, but I no longer drank over it. This process—even working with Amos, my sponsor—was a long and painful process. Slowly and carefully and with some discipline, I began to work through my anger at my parents and others by sharing and praying and meditating about these five basic points in the program.

The Fifth Step says: "Admitted to God, to ourselves and to another human being the exact nature of our wrongs." The word "wrongs" can be given a twelve-step program twist when we read further in the literature: "It is a spiritual axiom that every time we are disturbed, no matter what the cause, there is something wrong with us." In my anger, there has been something wrong with me, that I was angry and therefore upset. What was wrong is found in what my angry condition did to me. I even became angry about what the anger did to me. This is beyond being angry at Dad. I never found a way to right the wrong I felt—that I lost contact with my dad—so the anger came back into me. I was taken down by it, particularly when it got mixed up with my depression and my drinking.

When we came to step five, Amos asked me a question that sponsors have asked for a long time: "What haven't you told me as yet?" What I hadn't told him as yet were all those things about which I was embarrassed or wanted to keep private or thought should go down to the grave with me. I had bottled up so many bad feelings and resentment and down moods that it was stewing inside me as I was going down. Somehow, I opened up to Amos as I have never opened up to any other person, except Abraham and Lydia. There was for me something good about Amos, perhaps an honesty and trustworthiness that enabled me to do this. I became inclined to want to let go of everything with him. I was given a gift from my Higher Power, who is my God, to let those things out and to lay them out on the table for Amos to see and for us to share and examine, and to look at in the cool light of the day. The relief was tremendous. I felt that I could look the world in the eye. As the literature says: I felt as if "we were building an arch through we shall walk a free man at last."

Then I came to Step Six: "We're entirely ready for God to remove all these defects of character." I asked myself in amazement, *Could my defects of character be removed? Could I ever get beyond my deep anger and my specific resentments?* Good things began to happen to me when I shared these questions in meetings and talked to Amos about them and discussed them with Abraham. What would it mean for me to be free of the sort of anger that had plagued me so deeply? Why was I so deeply angry anyway?

At this point, I confronted a theme that has surfaced in this book—that is, that I came up as a boy into a man thinking that I wasn't worth much. This came from the reality of the situation in my early life when the only thing happening of any worth was what my dad was doing. It came from the almost total lack of parental encouragement of me in my career. It was the worry that nagged at me on a deep level most all my life.

It was especially in my counseling sessions with Abraham that I found out, as we discussed my lack of a sense of worth, that in practical ways this wasn't realistic. Under his sensitive guidance, *somehow the thought crept into my thick skull that I really was okay*! I felt the possibility that I was an okay, worthwhile, even special person. I had done worthwhile things. My self-esteem rose when it was pointed out to me that I had done valuable acts. After all, I had a good career with the sweet smell of success, had married a wonderful woman, and had three great children that are out in the world making contributions to society. They have closely knit families and smart and healthy children who are coming up in the same vein. To be sure, I was no big deal in society as was my dad, but what did that matter really? That was for him; I was okay as I was. I found out that I could stop worrying about myself so much. I discovered a link between me and anger in my sense of worthlessness. Once I got beyond that, a sweet relief swept over my consciousness.

Then I came to Step Seven: "Humbly asked Him to remove our shortcomings." I found that I could pray the seventh-step prayer: "My creator, I am now willing that you should have all of me, good and bad. I pray that you now remove from me every single defect of character which stands in the way of my usefulness to you and my fellows. Grant me strength as I go out from here to do your bidding." I had prayed for myself exactly what I wanted for myself, that is, a greater measure of freedom from my defects—from my anger and depression and my low self-esteem.

In praying this prayer, I found that I had done what I couldn't do before—that is, actually taking step three, "turning my will and life over to the care of God." I found that I could also pray the third-step prayer: "God, I offer myself to Thee—to build with me and do with me as Thou wilt; Relieve me of the bondage of self, that I may better do Thy will. Take away my difficulties so that victory over them may bear witness to those I would help of Thy power, Thy love, and Thy Way of life. May I do Thy will always!"

It came to me just what benefits these two prayers could mean to me and my life. Following them meant that I would no longer be caught in "the bondage of self." I would no longer—or not as much—be caught in the problem of selfishness and self-centeredness that were "the root of my problems." Working and living these middle steps of a twelve-step program from step three through step seven could mean that I would no longer be in a state where everything in life was about me or making me feel better. There could be a shift of emphasis from me to God, my Higher Power. There could be a shift from thinking of myself first to thinking of others and how in God's name I could be of some help to others. And the miracle is that in a large sense, this shift has indeed occurred in me during my period of recovery. Besides, there is the freedom to be able to think like this, as I have been "relieved of the bondage of self" in which I was caught in thinking of and worrying about myself as not of worth or value. I have in some good measure gotten beyond myself, freed for work with others for their betterment in sobriety.

There is a passage in the step three section that has made such a difference to me and my recovery. The passage reads in part:

> Selfishness—self-centeredness! That, we think is the root of our troubles. Driven by a hundred forms of fear, self-delusion, self-seeking, and self-pity, we step on the toes of our fellows and they retaliate ... So our troubles, we think, are of our own making. They arise out of ourselves and the alcoholic is an extreme example of self-will run riot ... Above all we alcoholics must be rid of this selfishness ... God makes that possible ... Many of us have had moral and philosophical convictions galore, but we could not live up to them even though we would have liked to. Neither could we reduce our self-centeredness much by wishing or trying on our own power. We had to have God's help.

One of my sponsees, named Michael, noted to me that my worn-out copy of a twelve-step work of literature had the back binding broken at the place between this passage and the third step prayer that I have already quoted. This passage and that prayer has made such a difference in my thinking during my recovery.

I see in myself that an absolutely main problem, an original sin in me, is found in my selfishness and self-centeredness. Something of that selfish condition has come out in me, and perhaps in my dad, in the sense of worthlessness or inferiority that Dad felt and that I have felt. As I now understand the program of recovery, it is of monumental importance that I turn away from inward selfish or self-centered thoughts and feelings toward thinking of others. As it says at another point in the literature of a twelve-step program, "Our very lives, as ex-problem drinkers, depend upon our constant thought of others and how we may help meet their needs."

So many times in a state of anger or worry or anxiety over myself, I take the practical turn of mind toward others and how I may perhaps be of some help to them. When I am able to focus on seeing how I can, perhaps, help meet their needs, I find a relief. But that's not it exactly. What I feel is a connection with God or my Higher Power, working in my life for the good of fellow alcoholics or needy persons in general.

When I was caught up in the "bondage of self," I was not able to make this spiritual switch in my mind and heart. Now in recovery, I have that power of choice, not only not to drink, but to turn outward with an attitude of being helpful to other still-suffering alcoholics. There is a creative movement in the spirits of the recovering alcoholic from selfishness, to turning my will and life over to the care of God, to a profound gratitude that I have been freed by my Higher Power from the grip of this selfishness and self-centeredness to a natural movement toward actions which may help other still-suffering alcoholics. Such is gratitude in action.

I came to Step Eight, a natural fault line in the process of working and living the steps. At this point, the recovering alcoholic works to clear his deck in his relations with others, particularly those he has "harmed." The eighth step reads: "Made a list of all people we had harmed, and became willing to make amends to them all." The first two people on my list were my dad and my mother.

First there is the case of Dad. I came to see that I had harmed him, in the sense of hurting him, as I sought and found my own way in life. That way for me was different from his way for him, and such that may well have troubled him. Dad may have asked himself, "Why wasn't my son following in my footsteps? Why is he so critical of me or disposed to be so critical all the time?" Critical has two important meanings here: first, perhaps, being negative and second, more in line with my philosophical sense, reflective and inclined to raise questions.

I realized how critical in the first sense that he thought I had been in many ways. For example, in one notable instance, Dad had been invited by his friend, President Richard Nixon, to be a minister to the boys in uniform by going to Vietnam and speaking and talking with them. From my anti-Vietnam War stance, I said that by going he would be giving at least a tacit approval to Nixon's policies in Vietnam. He said he was just going to "be a pastor to the boys." I suggested that this was naïve. To be sure, praying with the soldiers in Vietnam was not, in itself, a bad thing. Perhaps I was taking this opportunity to get back at Dad. At any rate, we started yelling at each other; I can't quite recall who was yelling the most. Mother came into the room and said to me, in her inimitable way, "You will not talk to your father like that." Without hesitation, I replied: "I will talk to my father in any damn way I please." This put my mother to silence, at least for the time being. Secretly, I had the idea that Dad liked this response, though he didn't show it.

I also figured that he had thought I was generally critical, and this became clear just to the extent that he was pleased and surprised at my Loews L'Enfant Hotel speech, in which I showed such an articulate and sensitive understanding and approval of the view of positive thinking.

So to be honest, I knew that I had to make amends to my dad. Of course, the eighth step says to first "become willing" to make amends. Amos and I talked about this. He helped me to realize that to be willing to make amends requires that one's thinking shifts from how the person in question has hurt me to how I have harmed that person. The wonder is that I found that such a psychological and spiritual shift had occurred in me to a good extent. Such are the benefits of a twelve-step program; such are the effects of much prayer and meditation; and in my case, such are the effects of good counseling by Abraham, my psychoanalyst. At any rate, I did shift and was ready to make amends in step nine.

The case of my mother was, in a sense, more difficult than that of my dad. This is due to the gatekeeper role she assumed in relation to her three children, and for that matter, everyone else. This role for Mother was a matter of the utmost importance to her. I think she took this role due to her decision that she needed to protect Dad and to create the maximally good conditions for him to do his work, for him to be creative and productive. I had to accept mother for what she was, not for the way I wanted her to be. This, of course, is a complicated and emotionally difficult matter.

Yet *I had become ready for Step Nine* after I completed the psychological healing process of having become willing to make amends. Step nine reads: "Made direct amends to such people wherever possible, except when to do so would injure them or others." It needs to be said that there were other people, besides my parents, on my step eight list. Mother and Dad are perhaps the most important in connection with this book, but of course, Lydia and our three children are of major importance to me also.

Since Dad passed away in 1993, seven or eight years earlier, I had the problem as to how I would make amends to him. Amos made the helpful suggestion that I send him a letter. I would be sending out from me my amends, an act that might have beneficial effects on me even if it couldn't on Dad. So I wrote a letter, put it into an envelope, sealed it, and on the outside of the envelope, I wrote nothing except the words "To My Dad." This letter probably ended up in a post office "dead letter" file somewhere. But I had sent it out and felt relieved in that effort.

I found that letter buried in old files on my computer and here it is.

> DEAR DAD: *You don't know this, I guess, but I am an alcoholic. Perhaps you could have or did know this. I arrived at this state, I know not when, but probably it was after you had passed away in December 1993. A good amount of my drinking was in a vain and self-defeating effort to medicate my emotions stirred up with the problems I had in our personal father-son relationship.*
>
> *There was a failure of monumental proportions in our relationship as there was only a very low level of genuine personal contact between you and me. I bitterly resented you for this most all my life, especially since I graduated from Deerfield. My resentments have been cleared away by working the wonderful and new-found steps of a twelve-step program, specifically step seven.*
>
> *Due to my character defects, I tried to hurt or harm you in many ways as a result of my angry reaction to your self-absorbed ways. I went to Union Theological Seminary with the one sentence letter you wrote me about this burned into my consciousness: "I can't understand why you are going into the seat of my most implacable enemies." I took considerable satisfaction in knowing that you felt as you did, that I had hurt you and got back at you.*

I went into academia, into philosophy as a field of interest and as a profession, and what in the hell is wrong with that? We had a big fight about Vietnam, and I said in anger as much as I could to hurt you on that occasion.

Of course, all the while I was doing all of these "harms" to you, I was seeking to gain closeness with you, which for me was a series of one failure after another. The biggest problem for me was that I sold my soul to praise you in my speeches, which were widely praised even by you, on the occasions of your 25th, 40th anniversaries from Marble and most notably at your funeral. I felt cheap and dishonest, and I went out and got drunk in a depressed stupor in the aftermath of these most difficult occasions.

I am willing, now, to make amends, and have been trying to do so for some time now with extensive and long-standing psychiatric counseling, not to mention my treatment for alcoholism, both in a twelve-step program and in the treatment center three-month program at Farley. My amends possibly will enable me to live a changed life, free of the chemical dependence of alcohol and living the kind of good life you would want of me anyway.

Love, John

In my counseling, I have recently experienced yet another significant breakthrough. This letter to Dad was written sometime in 2001, more than ten years ago. Now I see things quite differently from the way I felt back then. To explain this, I need to refer further to my counseling with Abraham. With him, I had worked through my anger, reporting it out with as little censorship as possible. This is what he suggested in our first meeting. He would help me draw connections in what I reported out. In the course of this process, it became clear that a major factor in my anger against Dad concerned the disturbing fact that I lost a personal connection with him and was worried and anxious about whether I would ever get it back. I have already discussed the first major breakthrough—that is, getting a live and realistic sense of my own worth as a person.

Abraham said to me something quite simple and amazingly well-timed. We talked about my personal loss of a close connection with my dad. He pointed out that *an appropriate response to such a potentially permanent loss was sadness more than anger.* Of course, anger and sadness can be known and shown together. But we began to focus on the sadness together over many sessions. Sadness is different from the type of anger I had. Sadness didn't seem to cut me off from other people, or isolate me as my own personal anger does. I could share my sadness with other people in similar situations. My own anger eating away at me from the inside out was my own self-destructive problem. I suffered from my anger; it was directed inwardly. I had directed anger outwardly, to be sure, and others suffered due to it. This is especially true of people I love most—my wife, Lydia, and three children, Laura, Cliff, and Lacy. I recall once Cliff said during my early recovery that he was so damn sick of my anger. With respect to my anger in myself, it was as if I were taking a big stick with which I intended to strike out at someone else and hitting myself over the head with it.

Sadness is different also from anger in being like the ebb and flow of the tides in the ocean. Many times, I have taken long reflective walks on the beach at the Outer Banks of North Carolina outside our beachfront home. I reflected on the sea—its constant movement, its beauty, its power. In and out, strong or weak, still or violent, it always is in a restless flow with alternating patterns of intensity. Sadness is like the ocean in many of these alternations. Besides, sadness feels so different from my violent anger. Sadness is quieter and more calm; anger was stronger and more agitating. To focus on the calm sadness became more central to me; the anger began to dissipate.

Step Ten says: "Continued to take personal inventory and when we were wrong promptly admitted it." Here one who is working and trying to live the steps enters the world of the spirit in a new way. The point here is that I would continue "to grow in understanding and effectiveness." Here I am directed to watch for "selfishness, dishonesty, resentment and fear. When these crop up, we ask God at once to remove them … We have ceased fighting anything or anyone—even alcohol. We are not cured of alcoholism. What we really have is a daily reprieve based on the maintenance of our spiritual condition. Every day is a day in which we must carry the vision of God's will into all our activities … It is the proper use of the will." As I have read, reread, and soaked in these words, my life has become calmer, more settled, more aligned with what I see as God's will in my life. I can't remember exactly when in more than twelve years of recovery I experienced, through my associations with Abraham, the conversion from an agitating anger to a quiet sadness. But that process happened and has settled into my consciousness. With the sadness, I am considerably less emotionally down than I ever was in the anger. Miraculous as it is, through the grace of God and within a twelve-step program, I have been able to go further into the action of really taking the third step, by more fully "turning my will and life over to the care of God."

However, I still had the nagging resentment against Mother, as I have already described. Ringing in the ears of my memory are the disturbing words in the literature that say, "Resentment is the number one offender. It destroys more alcoholics than anything else. From it stems all forms of spiritual disease ..." The literature also says that we had to be free of this anger, or we would die.

I had not been free of this anger, due to the ongoing resentment toward my mother. How could I get rid of it? I've prayed about this question, shared about it in twelve-step meetings, and talked to both Amos and Abraham. One day in Abraham's office, *there came another important revelation*, so simple now as I look back. I was talking about Mother, making some progress in gaining some balance in my emotional attitude toward her. I found myself saying to Abraham that there is this and that about her, which is good, "but ..." There was always the "but," and what followed the "but" was the negative resentment. Abraham suggested that I change the "but" to an "and."

Bells went off in my head, and the Sunlight of the Spirit showed through the darkness of my resentment. I could begin to see my mother not only as I resented her, but more as she was in herself. I could have a more balanced view of her as she was. I could see the agenda she had for helping her husband and the work she put into that. I could see it was that which was primary for her. And I actually began to accept that's the way she was. It was really okay that things were like that. I saw the many positive things she meant to me in my life. And so I became more fully relaxed. It was as if the weight of the resentment was falling from my shoulders. I stood up straighter and taller, with a clearer light in my eyes. The long-standing, nagging, and debilitating resentment began to give way in my heart. What a sweet relief it was. I walked out of Abraham's office with a new spring in my step. I shared all of this with Amos, and we took delight together.

Then I came to Step Eleven: "Sought by prayer and meditation to improve our conscious contact with God *as we understood Him*, praying only for knowledge of His will for us and the power to carry that out." I felt freed up again to feel the spirit in a way I had not been able to for a long, long time. I developed meditative and spiritual practices in my own life, in connection with a twelve-step program and in our church life at Westminster Presbyterian Church. Together with Amos, I talked over the reality and challenge of spiritual development in his life and in mine, often in the context of reading together helpful and significant literature, such as *The Spirituality of Imperfection* by Ernest Kurtz and Katherine Ketcham, and also *Will and Spirit* by Gerald May.

Lydia and I developed such practices together in our prayers and in readings before sleep every night. These have included spiritual literature from such people as Henri Nouwen. Most regularly, it focuses on readings from the Bible, from *Psalms for Praying*, by Nan C. Merrill, and also from a twelve-step program literature.

My spiritual sensitivities have been hugely enlarged and developed by regular attendance at twelve-step program meetings. Whether sharing or listening, I am an active participant in these meetings. At the time of this writing, I have attended well over four thousand twelve-step program meetings in the twelve years since March 11, 2000, almost one meeting a day for my entire recovery period. At so many meetings, the spiritual connection of us alcoholics is rich and focused. Meetings are so much more than psychological support groups. There is a spiritual presence from which we tap strength, comfort, and new perspectives on our living day by day.

Then, finally, *I came to Step Twelve*, which says: "Having had a spiritual awakening as the result of these steps, we tried to carry this message to alcoholics, and to practice these principles in all our affairs." In step twelve, we alcoholics step outward, out from our inner turmoil and desperation, out from our catching the Sunlight of the Spirit to pass on to other suffering alcoholics the message that we have been given. We turn outward with an attitude and disposition to be of some help in their own activity of coming to sobriety and of working and living the steps.

There is the promise of a "spiritual awakening" as we turn outward as recovering human beings to others, still-suffering alcoholics. For me, there had been at least the promise of having had a "spiritual awakening."

For me, the actual realization of this has been a miracle and a rich blessing. This is best described in a twelve-step program literature:

> When a man or a woman has a spiritual awakening, the most important meaning of it is that he has now become able to do, feel, and believe that which he could not do before on his unaided strength and resources alone. He has been granted a gift which amounts to a new state of consciousness and being. He has been set upon a path which tells him he is really going somewhere, that life is not a dead end, not something to be endured or mastered. In a very real sense he has been transformed, because he has laid hold of a source of strength which, in one way or another, he had hitherto denied himself. He finds himself in possession of a degree of honesty, tolerance, unselfishness, peace of mind, and love of which he had thought himself quite incapable. What he has received is a free gift, and yet usually, at least in some small part, he has made himself ready to receive it.

I have experienced a new spiritual awakening in my life in a twelve-step program and in general. My life is going in an increasingly different direction. I have taken steps to move outward, looking to think of others more than ever before, and praying to be able to cultivate an attitude of caring, accepting, and loving others. This has been focused on my work with my sponsees. I can also see this outward movement happening in me on a daily basis, with good results in my relation to Lydia, the children, colleagues, and so many other friends and associates.

Chapter 20: Becoming in My Pride for My Accomplishments

Now finally in my seventies, I can have pride for my accomplishments in life without bragging or being full of myself. I can also feel and express this pride without much of any resentment or bad feeling about my dad, and without comparing myself to him, though that often seems just beneath the surface of my consciousness.

I have had a good career, very satisfying, and rewarding for all the young college people I have taught, even those I never got to know very well, who perhaps didn't care or realized that they cared. I have received many letters from former students saying how much of an impact I had on their lives for the better, as the enrichment of their thought and character has sunk into their hearts and minds.

I feel that I was good in the classroom, for being in love with my subject matter of philosophy, for how I thought and learned myself, and very importantly, for how I cared about my students as they learned and developed. They knew that I cared about them. They knew that what I was teaching was important and important to me. They opened up and were touched not only intellectually, but also personally by me.

Perhaps there was something of my dad in me—something like what he felt when he preached. He cared about the people in the pews, and he spoke so well and with such power and good timing, with humor and conviction about the points he was making. I was like that in my classroom talks, with the people who were in my "congregation."

I too spoke with power and conviction with good timing and self-depreciating humor.

One of the emphases at Longwood University was service to students. In my work in campus activities, I was involved with students in important ways. With my engagement in work on the honor system, I was able to share my experience and wrestle with cases and issues before the student board, thus involving myself in the lives of students with whom I worked.

As I have written earlier, I have engaged in study all my adult life. In my "retirement," I am continuing that practice, working even better and more deeply on matters of concern and interest. My daily schedule might not be exactly up to that of Immanuel Kant, but I do still get up early, still under the influence of the daily pattern of Dr. Myers at Washington and Lee University, and do my own work in the morning hours before the busyness of the day begins.

With the freedom from working at a scheduled day-to-day job, I can explore what interests me and get into it as much as I like. A staple in this work is my Chinese studies, my papers on Chinese philosophers, many of which I present at academic meetings, fleshing out themes in my book about Christianity in China and learning considerably more about Chinese thought and culture in its language, history, philosophy, and religion.

There are many other examples. In the spring of 2010, Lydia and I took a trip to Eastern Europe for our fiftieth-wedding anniversary, cruising down the Danube River from the Black Forest to the Black Sea, and I was shocked to realize how much I didn't know about that part of the world. So I bought a book by Norman Davies that I have now read, *Europe: A Panorama of Europe, East and West, from the Ice Age to the Cold War, from the Urals to Gibraltar.* This book has 1,136 pages of text, and an additional 229 pages of notes, charts, and graphs.

When the 150-year anniversary of John Calvin's birthday came up recently, I read the whole of the *Institutes of the Christian Religion*, edited by John T. McNeill and translated by Ford Lewis Battles in volumes XX and XXI of the famed Library of Christian Classics.

As it happened, my interest in Ernest Hemingway got reawakened, and I read several of his novels, some of his short stories, and a quite exciting literary biography of Hemingway by the noted author Kenneth S. Lynn (yet another 700-plus-page book).

Another example is that of T. E. Lawrence, who was made into "Lawrence of Arabia" by Lowell Thomas and by the notable movie by the same name. When I was a boy, I knew Lowell Thomas personally on Quaker Hill at the summer home of my parents. I took on the book entitled *Hero: The Life and Legend of Lawrence of Arabia*, by Michael Korda, and as I write, I am well into a reading of *Seven Pillars of Wisdom*, the great book by Lawrence. I find him a most intriguing character and am fascinated by the details and the broad stokes of such an exciting life, even with the ending some call tragic.

And in our book groups, Lydia and I together read the sorts of books that I don't ordinarily spend my time with, such as our current novel, *Caleb's Crossing* by Geraldine Brooks. We read a wide assortment of books on politics, international relations, religion, philosophy, history, and also fiction, with good friends who are growing old together with us.

The mornings of this writer are spent alternating involvement with all these things mentioned, and I keep a record in a journal of what I have done and what it has meant to me.

Our family life is settled and creative and fun, especially between me and Lydia on a day-to-day basis, being loving together and engaging in an interesting life together. We are actively involved in the lives of our three children and their families, with frequent telephone calls to Lebanon, New Hampshire, to our daughter Laura and her family; to Covington, Kentucky, to our son, Clifford, and his family; and to Arlington, Virginia, to our daughter Lacy and her three-year-old fun, little boy named Jake. Jake was adopted by Lacy three years ago. It is a great delight to watch him grow into an active little boy.

Lydia and I have many good friends with whom we relate easily and happily on a daily basis. I have a host of friends who care about me and about whom I care. In a twelve-step program these especially include people who are in regular attendance with me in program meetings and particularly my twelve-step program sponsees, with whom I have spent so many hours of sharing and guidance in the program. With me the sponsees, as well as the sponsor, gains so much from these helpful sessions. My sponsees are named Sam, Michael, Brad, Kenny, Antwan, and Vince and my sponsor, Amos. My life in this twelve-step program is active, and I go to meetings regularly. In twelve plus years, I have been averaging between six and seven meetings each week, together with my reading of the literature, my working on the steps, and my meditation and prayers.

And I write, especially now, on papers on philosophical subjects, widely conceived. Recently, I have been particularly productive in the area of Chinese studies, with my book, *The Love of God in China: Can One Be Both Chinese and Christian*. Later work on numerous Chinese philosophers is on my writing agenda. Often I go back to my book written in 1985, entitled *Biblical History as the Quest for Maturity*. This helps to bring to the fore in my mind and heart topics I formerly engaged in, which I can make current in my present life.

Naturally there is always the thought of my writing compared to that of my dad. This book that you are reading is only my third book; the number of Dad's books totals forty-six. This contrast is fine with me, and as they say today, "no problem." Once when I was young, I half-kiddingly told Dad that he said the same thing in each of his forty-six books. In no way do I wish to deprecate the enormous value of these books, particularly the help that they have been to so many people. I believe I made that point clear in the talk I gave at the Celebration of the Life of Norman Vincent Peale, in December 1993—as present in my first interlude in this book.

My children never told me that I said the same things in my books, as I told my dad. I doubt that my children have read my books; at any rate, that is their business and not mine. My son Cliff did say that he once checked the works of me and that of his grandfather in a bibliography. He found the following contrast: they had from me a book entitled *Biblical History and the Quest for Maturity*, and for Dad, they had a book called *Have a Nice Day*. Clifford thought this was amusing, as do I. At any rate, the contrast and comparison is fine with me.

I have the opportunity to spend time with Abraham, my psychiatrist, whom I have been seeing for longer than I have been sober, and with whom I have a close personal connection. Lydia sometimes openly wonders about my talking sports with my psychiatrist. I kid him openly about the models of clarity in his analysis when I believe him to be unclear, and I suggest that I might report him to the national psychiatric association—if there is such an organization—for his actually suggesting something practical that I might do! When I first met him, he suggested that I report out to him what was on my mind with as little censorship as possible and he would help me draw connections. Right away, I suggested that he change his suggestion to what was on my mind and heart. Our sessions are mentally full of understanding and emotionally full of heart, with mutual respect a constant factor.

On a regular but not a daily schedule, I have sessions with Amos, usually over coffee and always with a rich sense of mutual appreciation for each other and for the blessings that have come to each of us due to our recovery programs. It is so special to connect personally, even transparently, in our respective journeys to a higher level of spiritual and psychological health. Each of us is an agent for the spiritual health of the other. What a blessing!

Due to what we have earned, and due in no small measure to the financial planning and generosity of my mother and dad, Lydia and I can live in relative comfort. Lydia and I have basically all we want, and our lives are open to numerous interesting and diverse pursuits.

I wanted to be like Dr. Myers, and I have done that. I wanted to love my dad and be like him, yet be me, finding my own way—and I have done that. The kind of happiness I feel is at times something like that of contentment reached by the ancient Chinese philosopher Confucius.

Chapter 21: Being Me

*"At seventy I could give my heart-and-mind free rein
without overstepping the mark."*
—Confucius, *Analects* 2/4

Being Me in the Now

In my midseventies, the major conflicting strands in my life have become largely resolved. I am no longer trying to find my own way in life, adjusting to what I have wanted to do and be, with my sense of the influence of my dad in my life. Being the son of Norman Vincent Peale is now a new, proud, and considerably more peaceful factor in my life. There is nothing more I need to worry about concerning my position as the son of a famous father. I am now me—and happy about it. As stated in the quotation about a spiritual awakening in the twelve-step program, I have, in a real sense, become a new me! I can reaffirm what I said in my talk at the Celebration of the Life of Norman Vincent Peale service at Marble Collegiate Church in 1993, when I loved Dad but was of a divided mind and heart. What I said was that if I am worthy, and if it be God's will, there will come the time when I will again be with him in God's eternal presence. Perhaps in that next life the resolution can become completed.

In me, there has been a passage from feeling worthless to realizing that I am okay, even special as a person. There is some considerable peace in me about this. I am not famous as was Dad, and frankly that is just fine with me. As I wrote, I am proud of my accomplishments in life, and I am happy each day I have with Lydia and my family and friends, living in a most interesting place, and with the energy to do good things with good people in life. I am an intellectual, valuing the life of the mind, introduced as I was by Dr. Myers of Washington and Lee University so long ago.

My experience and my life in a twelve-step program have shown me, however, that humility is more important than intellect. In a twelve-step program literature, regarding step two, it is said that some people are intellectually self-sufficient. For them, "the god of intellect displaced the God of our fathers ... We found many in ... who once thought as we did. They helped us to get down to our right size. By their example they showed us that humility and intellect could be compatible, provided we placed humility first. When we began to do that, we received the gift of faith, a faith which works."

What is most important to me is being of help to other people, of not placing me in a more prominent place in my heart and mind than others are in.

I also have made progress in *forgiving my dad and my mother.* What a spiritually settling factor this has become! I now can see them, not only as I have resented them, but also as they were in themselves, with all their shortcomings and their own agenda for their lives and work. The psychological and spiritual breakthrough when I could change the "but" in my descriptions of my mother to an "and" was a major step in coming to this forgiveness, as was the coming to value myself as a person, and the conversion from my anger at Dad to the state of sadness. I have let go of my specific resentments, no longer dwelling on them but thinking of them as a past reality. The deep anger that ate away at me is largely dissipated. I no longer feel this way anymore, as I have changed significantly through a twelve-step program and my sharing at meetings, with Amos, and in my counseling with Abraham.

To say that I have forgiven my parents is not quite right. What is on the mark is that I have become fully willing to forgive them, and perhaps that is all that I or anyone can do. I believe that it is God who forgives. It is enough that I have experienced the spiritual blessings of a change of attitude, which has allowed me to see them in a balanced way. As it says in a twelve-step program literature: "God has done for me what I cannot do for myself."

I feel that it is not we who forgive other persons on our own unaided strength and wisdom. Some higher power is necessary here, some power to forgive, not in me alone. I can let resentments go, I can see people in a more balanced way, I can even wish them well, and I can adjust my feelings in so doing. And it is these things that compose the action called forgiving. What I need to do is to be willing to forgive, like becoming willing to make amends. Once I am willing, good things happen. I believe that I also have to turn the other person over to God, praying for them as I would pray for myself. Following that, I believe, the real forgiveness comes. It is God who forgives.

In my early twenties, I was angered by the fact that I had lost close personal contact with my dad. Life was a struggle between developing my own life and being so frustrated and angry about my dad and my parents. That struggle is now over; being torn apart has been replaced by being whole, or more so. That has happened, not as a result of my efforts, but in the context of God's grace.

Weight control is one ongoing aspect of my recovery that I have not yet mentioned. This is relevant and important to the recovery work that I have done. In 1997, at the height of my active alcoholism, my weight had mushroomed up until I tipped the scales at 259.6, this on a frame of only five feet nine inches. This was not good. Even in that condition, I was able to make a good decision to try to do something about my weight. As I have said earlier in this book, my dad's weight also mushroomed up until he was very thick around the middle. It was the same for me in 1997.

I decided to put myself in the hands of licensed nutritionists at the University of Virginia Medical Center, beginning in December 1997. I have kept up that routine with regular visits for more than thirteen years. During that time, I have lost seventy-five pounds, and what is even better, I have maintained a weight of no higher than the mid-180s for more than a decade. I have learned to count calories and to adjust what I eat so that the intake of food is healthy and light, day after day. Each morning, I weigh myself and make adjustments in my diet, and each month, I visited my nutritionist, until I was released by my last professional, named Mary Lou, in 2010.

During all this time, I kept a diet and health journal for every day, since the end of 1997, of what I ate plus a calorie-count estimate of that food, together with a record of the amount of water intake and exercise. I am now on volume twenty-six of my set of notebooks on this journal! Mary Lou said that if I were to throw away my notebook and stop being accountable to my records, and stop my regular exercise, then I would willy-nilly gain weight back in a big hurry. This seems precisely parallel with the idea of abstinence in my recovery as an alcoholic. If I were to stop going to the twelve-step program meetings and stop working the program in my daily life, I would willy-nilly go back to where I was in the spring of 2000. This would happen very fast, and I would be the same off now as I was then—or probably worse. The progressive nature of the disease of alcoholism would show itself big time.

So my recovery has this dual character. It is about eating and exercising and being healthy physically, and it is about praying and meditating, working the program, and being healthy psychologically and spiritually. I intend and expect and hope that I will be carrying on these two activities until the day I die.

When I turned seventy-three, I celebrated my tenth anniversary of sobriety in a twelve-step program. My wife, Lydia, was proud, as were all three of my children. Clifford came to the twelve-step meeting where I received my ten-year medallion. It meant so much to me that he drove all the way from Kentucky to Virginia to be with me on this occasion. It was so apparent that my relationship to my family then and in my seventies is free of so many deep conflicts.

I have developed a spiritual and psychological maturity, which has led to a largely steady contentment on my own. After working through my anger and depression, especially in a twelve-step program's steps four and five and the rest of the steps, I have come to a good place in my life.

Being Me: The Promise of the Future

The Confucian view of "free rein" of mind and heart without overstepping the mark can be given an interpretation of my life in a twelve-step program, based on the ninth-step promises. I also feel like Confucius when he called "the Master" and said: "Let me live a few more years so that I will have had fifty years of study in which after all I will have remained free of any serious oversight" (*The Analects of Confucius*, 7:17). Confucius said also that he had come to a time in life when he could do what he pleased.

Insofar as I devote myself to the realization of these promises in my life, I will have, like Confucius, "free rein" of mind and heart "without overstepping the mark." Or so I believe. When asked, "Are these extravagant promises?" people in a twelve-step program then say,

"We think not." I think not also. I think that if I keep working for the realization of these twelve promises in my life, they will come true.

This prediction is a promise made about these twelve promises in the literature of a twelve-step program. It is stated that these promises "are being fulfilled among us—sometimes quickly, sometimes slowly. They will always materialize if we work for them." And ringing in our ears in the background is the statement in an earlier chapter entitled "How it Works": "Rarely have we seen a person fail who has thoroughly followed our path." It is affirmed that "We are not saints. The point is that we are willing to grow along spiritual lines. The principles we have set down are guides to progress. We claim spiritual progress rather than spiritual perfection."

Besides the ninth-step promises, there is one other affirmation that I will make at the end of this chapter and this book: What I have in my sobriety, what I have become in it, and what will come in the future is a fragile and priceless gift. It is wise to focus on emotional and spiritual sobriety as a gift, one that comes out of the goodness and benevolence of a power greater than myself—my Higher Power. It is realistic to focus on this gift as fragile—that is, delicate and breakable—and priceless, meaning valuable in and of itself, in the extreme.

The Ninth-Step promises:

> We are going to know a new freedom and a new happiness. We will not regret the past nor wish to shut the door on it. We will comprehend the word serenity and we will know peace. No matter how far down the scale we have gone, we will see how our experience can benefit others. That feeling of uselessness and self-pity will disappear. We will lose interest in selfish things and gain interest in our fellows. Self-seeking will slip away. Our whole attitude and outlook upon life will change. Fear of people and of economic insecurity will leave us. We will intuitively know how to handle situations which used to baffle us. We will suddenly realize that God is doing for us what we could not do for ourselves.

In my spiritual awakening, as a result of working and living the steps, *I have and I will come to know a freedom and happiness that is new,* one I had not had for oh so long—I can't really even say how long. My consciousness is no longer so fractured and divided by my anger and depression, which were so hurtful to me and to those around me. The onset of this new happiness and new freedom has been a gradual thing, as I have worked for them. It needs to be stressed that in the life of recovery, the primary goal is not for me to become happy. What I strive for is my physical, emotional, and spiritual sobriety, always thinking of carrying the message to the still-suffering alcoholic and not aiming at my own happiness. Wonderful it is that such happiness usually does come, like a by-product of the quest for the best kind of sobriety.

I will not regret the past nor wish to shut the door on it. The past has weighed me down and weighs down alcoholics in recovery. It was such a blessing one day when I awoke to realize that I had this new freedom and new happiness and that I could see the past for what it was and not psychologically need to "shut the door on it." I could learn from it and move on. Crucial to this realization is the fact that somehow, I really know not how, I really have gotten beyond the shame and the guilt. I will never forget what Phil told me that awful yet good morning when I was dissolved in tears at a twelve-step program meeting, just after hitting my bottom. It is absolutely amazing, explainable only by the grace of God, my Higher Power, and my work in my recovery program, that this new relaxed and accepting attitude about my wreckage of my past has changed me. The past is present in my vivid memory of just how bad it was back then—something I never want to know again in the remainder of my life.

The promise is made to me that *I will come to "comprehend the word serenity,"* that is, to know a new and greater peace and contentment in my life, most all the time. If it is not adequate to hear this from me in my writing; just ask my wife, Lydia, and the rest of my family, and see what they say. Again, this serenity and peace is not a possession I can grab onto and hold. It too is a by-product of my years of working and living in the program, and its continuance is contingent on the further work I will be doing in the twelve-step program the rest of my life. How many times I have prayed the Serenity Prayer, which says: "God, grant me the serenity to accept the things I cannot change, the courage to change the things I can, and the wisdom to know the difference." We alcoholics internalize this prayer and pray it constantly, even when we are not consciously thinking about it.

No matter how far down the scale we have gone, we will see how our experience can benefit others. In the past, as I have shown, I went pretty far down the scale of living at the time of my bottom and the years leading up to that terrible time. My bottom had gotten lower in the dark, bottomless pit into which I was going down at my bottom time. But it is such a blessing to behold how I and other alcoholics can use these experiences to be of benefit to others. We can get the confidence of another suffering alcoholic in but a short time as we share our experience, strength, and hope with them, showing that we were where they are in their present suffering. This is the basis of the great help a sponsor can be to a sponsee who is still suffering.

That feeling of uselessness and self-pity will disappear. Amazing as it seems, that feeling will slip away and dissipate from my consciousness. Oh how I used to pity myself, saying, "Why me?"—asking and bemoaning how I got into the down-and-out state of my being. The seemingly miraculous fact is that I, who was sinking into that dark space where I felt alone and with no support or stability, can be of use to others who are desperate themselves. Instead of pitying myself, I can think of myself as an agent of hope in the lives of others, maybe. I can be ready to carry the message and be a beacon of the Sunlight of the Spirit that can pierce the darkness of other suffering alcoholics. What a wonderful opportunity.

We will lose interest in selfish things and gain interest in our fellows ... [that] self-seeking will slip away." We affirm these promises and say with each other that this promise is not extravagant. Beg your pardon. Every time I affirm that with gusto, I say to myself that it is a most "extravagant" promise indeed. I started my life as an alcoholic, thinking that life was all about me. I took myself as the center of the universe. Everything I did was designed to make me feel better. Then I started to work the steps of my chosen twelve-step program, and my whole attitude in life began to change.

It is absolutely amazing that I, self-centered and selfish to the extreme, am now able to think so much of other still-suffering alcoholics and care about them, seeking to be of some help in their own journey toward a good sobriety.

Our whole attitude and outlook upon life will change. What a beautiful promise. As an alcoholic, my attitude was one of selfishness and self-centeredness, as everything I did and wanted to do concerned making myself feel better, changing my mood from hurting to being able to forget that or lose a sense of the emotional pain. After working the steps in a twelve-step program, my attitude has changed, and my outlook has shifted so that I am looking outward to others and looking forward for opportunities to be of some help to the still-suffering alcoholic, especially my sponsees and my colleagues in our fellowship. The realization of this promise will be a main basis for the hope that I have in life.

In fact, my whole attitude and outlook on life has changed. When I was young in sobriety, I was suffering in myself and my anger and depression and darkness and desperation. When I was at my bottom, it finally sunk into my thick skull that I needed to change some things in my life. Efforts in that direction were so difficult and painful. In the end, I realized that what I needed to do was to change everything about myself. Of course, I could not do that on my own unaided strength. But in my life, in a twelve-step program over the past twelve years, everything has changed, and in some measure, I have a new state of consciousness or being. That is a major blessing of the twelve-step program, dependent entirely upon my work, yes, but mostly on the Higher Power that I have tapped into and on the grace of God.

Fear of people and of economic insecurity will leave us. It is the fear part of this statement that is crucial. Fear is an unwanted and pervasive factor in the lives of alcoholics. It is that "evil and corroding thread, the fabric of our lives was shot through with it." For me, it is the fear of other people that has been the hardest nut to crack open. I have come to realize, oh so painfully, that I can accept other people the way they are, to give them space to be themselves and to let them be themselves.

Today, so many are paralyzed by the fear of financial insecurity. The antidote of fear is faith—faith in that Higher Power that can pull us up out of that morass of suffering that we alcoholics know so well. I need the maintenance of a vital sense of my Higher Power or God in my life to be able to say that this and these fears have left me. And that sense is most available to me when I am in a disposition to be of help to others.

We will intuitively know how to handle situations which used to baffle us. I can intuitively know how to handle difficult and stressful and desperate situations that used to baffle me and get me down into the depths. For example, I used to get upset by so many little things, such as interruptions of my precious routines or something happening that causes me to have to focus on something else that doesn't seem as important at the moment as what I am doing for myself.

We will suddenly realize that God is doing for us what we could not do for ourselves. The major factor in all of this is to realize that God is doing for me what I could not do for myself. My sobriety is based on maintenance of my spiritual condition. This is a day-by-day thing. To be able to look outward to satisfy the genuine needs and wants of others for their own sake is a gift of my Higher Power that takes me out of myself and makes me useful and whole in service to others.

In the end stands that ideal of what we call the St. Francis Prayer, which opens up the possibility of something perhaps so contrary to our natures: "self-forgetting." We who were thinking only of ourselves can now forget ourselves in the aim to be of service to others. The grace of God is abundant in my life and the lives of so many alcoholics who know of what I now write.

As one of my Charlottesville twelve-step colleagues and friends named Derrick is wont to say: "It is alcohol-ism not alcohol-wasim." And I am led to Derrick's favorite passage in the literature of a twelve-step program:

> It is easy to let up on the spiritual program of action and rest on our laurels. We are headed for trouble if we do, for alcohol is subtle foe. We are not cured of alcoholism. What we have is a daily reprieve based on the maintenance of our spiritual condition. Every day is a day when we must carry the vision of God's will into all of our activities. How can I best serve Thee—Thy will (not mine) be done. These are the thoughts which must go with us constantly. We can exercise our will power along this line all we wish. It is the proper use of the will.

I have a friend named Lyn Price of Oklahoma who has, with a smile on his face, referred to my being in the shadow of Norman Vincent

Peale. I never thought about it that way, exactly. Instead it was my finding my own way that mattered most. I had to live in the tension that I have described, which was difficult to do in relation to Dad and Mother. The crucial personal problems I had in relation to Dad have largely been resolved in my heart. I feel that I have come out from what Lyn and others perceived as the shadow into the Sunlight of the Spirit. If Lyn or anyone else chooses to see me in Dad's shadow, that is fine with me. However, for me, I have come out of that state into the light.

In my reflections on becoming at the beginning of this book, I constructed a music analogy, according to which I have experienced a love/death experience with Dad. This is analogous to the "Liebestod" at the conclusion of Wagner's opera, *Tristan und Isolde*. I have loved Dad all my life, but there was a death of our personal connection. I have come back to life in my own recovery, and I still look for a recovery of the lost connection with my dad, perhaps in the life to come. As I have said, maybe, if I am worthy, and if we are worthy, and if it be God's will, there will come the day when we too will rejoin him in God's eternal presence. This I firmly believe.

W*hat I have in my sobriety, what I have become in it, is a fragile and priceless gift.* It is fragile, for it is not something I have or possess, and I could lose it in the twinkling of an eye with that first drink. There is in me a sense that given certain conditions that might come into my life, I could and would drink again. If that happened, I have the firmly established belief that it would just be a matter of time—and very little time at that—before I would be back where I was when I hit my bottom in the spring of 2000, or even worse. After all that I have been through, I would have to have yet another recovery in me, and that is too painful even to contemplate.

So my psychological and spiritual recovery is conditional on my continuing to do all those things I have come to do in my twelve years of sobriety. I need to continue to throw myself into a twelve-step program in all its aspects—meetings of the fellowship, working and living the steps, meetings with Amos and my sponsees, times of meditation and prayer, and most importantly being available and disposed to carry the message to the still-suffering alcoholic.

What I have now is priceless, the most valuable thing in my life. As we alcoholics say, anything I would put before my sobriety I am liable to lose. Any other and every other value for me is secondary to the value of the sort of sobriety I am now endeavoring to describe. It is priceless, beyond measure.

It also is a gift to me, a free gift of inexhaustible power that has come to me. That I can tap into this power supply is not of my own doing, but of the grace of God, my Higher Power, together with my own work in recovery. It has pulled me up out of the morass of my drunken state. In working and living the twelve-step program, I have felt and experienced the grace of God or of my Higher Power and that has been electric. Due to God's grace and to my work in the twelve-step program, I am a person who sees the Sunlight of the Spirit in my life—one day at a time.

Epilogue

J ust how far am I from the apple tree? How much or how far am I from
my dad? It seems that answers to such questions will differ according
to the perspective of the person who wishes to ask and answer these
questions. In the end, it will be up to the reader to answer the question
as to just how far I am from the apple tree.

Dad was a practical man of enormous talents and strong desires to
be helpful to other people in the name of his faith, in what he called
the life-saving presence of the Lord Jesus Christ. In his work, he
formed his view of the power of positive thinking and promoted that
work from the publication of his book of that title in 1952 until his
death in 1993. He did this in so many diverse ways, giving testimony
to his enormous talents in the various aspects of his ministry over his
professional career from the 1920s to the 1990s.

Many people see him as being enormously successful and are
highly respectful in their admiration and praise. I am like this also.
Such people, perhaps, may not see me as following in my father's
footsteps. They see that I am not a church minister, although I am
ordained a minister in the Reformed Church. They are aware that I
do not work in all the Peale business enterprises.

I refer here particularly to the Guideposts organization. In this
connection, I regularly attend and participate in the National Advisory
Cabinet (NAC) of Guideposts. The NAC is a group of active supporters
of Guideposts from around the country who help in promoting its
various programs and ministries. It may seem to some that my two
sisters are more actively carrying on the message and the work of NVP

than am I. By some, I may be viewed as having fallen away from the apple tree.

There is a family foundation, named the Peale Foundation, and I am one of the three directors, together with my two sisters. I am actively involved in Peale Foundation business, as I have been since its inception in the early 1990s. The Foundation offers the rich promise of carrying on the work of my dad in a new day.

All my life, in meeting people who identify me as the son of Norman Vincent Peale, I have been able to sense a difference among such persons. Obviously there are those that see me as the son of the famous and enormously popular Norman Vincent Peale. Understandably, this is their focus. They don't see me as a person in my own right, don't intuitively connect with me in my difficult relation to my famous father. On the other hand, there are some who express sensitivity to my personal life of having come through that experience of being NVP's son. There may be ardent supporters of my dad who see me as having rolled some distance away from the apple tree.

Norman Vincent Peale lived and preached a practical Christianity. Although it is said that he read voraciously and was certainly well-educated, he did not have a comfortable relationship with scholars or those in the academic life. In this area, he seemingly always felt inferior. This was the area in which his "inferiority complex" kicked in most clearly.

As I have written extensively in this book, I have become a professor of philosophy with a mostly successful teaching and scholarly career. Since Dad felt uncomfortable in the scholarly and academic arenas, and since I am so involved there, it is natural that I may be viewed as having fallen far from the apple tree. As Dad was a thoroughly practical man, and as I have been a teacher, philosopher, and scholar, it may suggest to some a distance between me and the apple tree.

There is another sense that for me is crucial in the discussion of how far away I may have fallen. This is the matter of an emotional and loving and respectful stance that I have in my heart and mind about my dad. He and I loved each other all our lives. That is for sure. Readers of this book will have noted the first sentence of my first section on my becoming, "Becoming in loving and being loved." In that section, I wrote the following: "In my life, I have enjoyed the good fortune of loving Dad and of having been loved by him from boyhood days to his death on December 24, 1993, at the age of ninety-five." I believe that in my love for him and his love for me, we were close, despite all my talk of our troubling disconnection after my high school years. The fact of this love places me not far at all from the apple tree.

I respect and share much of what I got from Dad indirectly—that is, a sense of humor, my speaking ability, a natural way of connecting with other people, and a valuing of family tradition.

In the ending chapters of the book, I have made much of my recovery from alcoholism and my work in a twelve-step program. For me, working with other alcoholics, especially my sponsor and my sponsees, is not unlike teaching or pastoral ministry, both of which have been bred into me all my professional life, as a minister and an experienced teacher and professor. I believe that Dad would be proud of me for that if he were here to see me as I am now, so different from when he knew me before he died.

In this connection, I would like to return to the talk I gave at the Celebration of the Life of NVP service at Marble Church on December 29, 1993, just five days after Dad died. In that talk and in that service, I poured out myself in genuine feeling and love and respect for Dad, and I was proud of showing just who he was and how great he was in the world. Although I pitched that talk in an earlier context of feeling the loss of my personal connection with Dad, I meant everything I said and was proud of the way I said it. In an emotional and spiritual sense, that speech stands in my heart and mind as a testimony to how much I loved him and valued him and wanted to be close to him. When people see me as they saw me at that time, I feel comfortable in the thought that despite everything, I am not so far from the apple tree.

In this book, it has been shown in great detail how I suffered with the belief that I can be close to Dad or to anyone else—even with such distinct and clear differences between us. It has been a big problem for me that Dad didn't share this view, especially across the divides that seemed to separate us. That is still painful, yet I have come to see as a problem that I have had to bear as a loving and dutiful son.

I end this epilogue with the sentiment, dear to me, which I have already quoted from the end of my talk at the Celebration of the Life of NVP on December 29, 1993. There I affirm, as I also did in reference to the "Liebestod" of Wagner's *Tristan und Isolde*, that the story is not over. In the life to come, it is my hope that the loss of personal contact with my dad can somehow be overcome.

Finally, in dealing with the question set in the title of this book—*Just How Far from the Apple Tree?*—I suggest that you, the reader, be the judge for me. And more importantly, for yourself.

Index

References to "NVP" refer to Norman Vincent Peale
Books referenced as "(Peale)" refer to Norman Vincent Peale
Books referenced as "(Peale, J.)" refer to John S. Peale

179